Setting for "Opal's Million Dollar Duck"

Opal's Million Dollar Duck

BY JOHN PATRICK

★

DRAMATISTS
PLAY SERVICE
INC.

SOUND EFFECTS

The following is a list of sound effects referenced in this play:

Car starting, and pulling away

OPAL'S MILLION DOLLAR DUCK was first presented by the School of Performing Arts, Inc., in St. Thomas, U.S. Virgin Islands, on September 16, 1979. It was directed by the author; the assistant to the director was John Corey; the set designer was William Walstrum; the stage manager was Sally Harkness; and the "Mallard Masterpiece" was by John Suydam. The cast was as follows:

OPAL ....Marye Brent

ROSIE ....Marjorie Austrian

DESMOND (KING) ....Walter Williamson

QUEENIE ....Rhoda Rosen

Opal's Million Dollar Duck

ACT ONE

Time: *The present.*

Place: *The living room of Opal's ancient Victorian house at the edge of the municipal dump on the outskirts of the city. It has peeling wallpaper and broken banisters leading to the rooms above. There is a ramp on the stairs where Opal's toy wagon full of junk is pulled up by a rope and pulley.*

With its assortment of piled up newspapers, books, boxes, barrels, tires, stuffed animals, and broken statuary, the room is a collector's dream.

There is a sagging, discarded sofa, a table and several risky chairs.

In an alcove u.l. there is a clothesline, on which Opal hangs her teabags to dry. Below this is a rusty kerosene stove with kettle.

A door l. leads to the kitchen.

A crude sign below the stair proclaims:

"OPALS ANTIQUE JUNQUE SHOP"

At Rise: *After the audience has had time to absorb the bizarre scene, Opal enters the front door, r.*

She pulls a child's wagon with salvaged treasures. She kicks the door closed behind her, singing tunelessly "Dum-de-dum-dum, Driftwood."

Her face is almost hidden by a man's floppy hat and a moth-eaten scarf several feet long. She is bundled in a large overcoat that hangs to the floor.

Still humming, she takes a rolled-up painting from the wagon and places it on the table. She then hauls the wagon upstairs after hitching it to the rope pulley.

She then turns to the business of taking off scarf, three overcoats, leaving only a knee-length sweater.

She then trudges up to the alcove, and pours hot water into a tin cup from the kettle on top of the kerosene stove. She dips the cup up and down under one of the bags without removing it from the line, humming all the while.

She then crosses to the table, to blow into her cup and enjoy her tea.

5

She unrolls the painting and looks at it. She then turns to the audience and looks at them.

OPAL. (*To audience.*) You wanna see sumpin? (*Holds canvas so that the audience can see it. It is an oil painting of a Mallard duck hanging on a bare wall. On the table below is a lone apple in a plain dish.*) You like it? Found it in the alley behind the Hockenheimer Museum on Pussywillow and Coolidge. They'd throw'd it away. Can't say I blame 'em. I shore wouldn't want no dead duck hangin' on my wall while I was tryin' eat my liver. Wonder why it got painted in the first place? Musta bin a pet. But why do you suppose that there painter feller put a apple in? Musta bin his lunch. Wouldn't surprise me, after he'd finished his painting, he et both his *subjects*. Artists is famous for starvin to death. Seems like they have to die before they're appreciated. Well, that's true of most of us. Kinda sad that poor painter feller only had a dead duck to paint—couldn't afford no nude lady, I guess. Still an' all, he wuz proud of it—signed his name. (*Reads.*) Van—Von—Vander somethin'. Sounds Puerto Rican. Only they paint fish. Oh, well— somebody'll come along likes ducks an' buy it. Ef I wait long enough, an' the mice don't git to it. (*She has just rolled up the painting, when the door bursts open and Rosie Montefalco, Opal's friend, races in. She is a rather dumpy Italian in a black dress and attitude.*)

ROSIE. Opal! It's you! You're alive!

OPAL. Rosie Montefalco—you bin tellin' my fortune with them cards again?

ROSIE. Yes! And you come up dead three times. (*Takes off coat.*) An' before breakfast, too.

OPAL. Well, I'm sorry to disappoint you, dearie. I'll be around long after them cards is gone.

ROSIE. My cards don't lie, Opal. Somebody is tryin' to git thru to you to warn you about somethin'. You bin takin' your vitamins? (*Makes self a cup of tea.*)

OPAL. My old Gran-Mother Kronkie never *heard* of vitamins in her whole entire life. An' *she* lived to be a hundred and five, six months, three days an' twenty minutes.

ROSIE. (*Returns to sit with Opal.*) The Bible says "in the midst of life our number may be next." So do my cards. I jes' hope you'll still be alive on my next birthday.

OPAL. When is that?

ROSIE. Friday.

6

OPAL. Well, now, I'm glad you tole me, dearies. I'll have to dig out a present fer you.

ROSIE. No—no! I don't want you to go to no trouble.

OPAL. No trouble. Yore my bes' fren', Rosie.

ROSIE. Don't matter. I don't want *nobody* to give me *no* presents. That's final.

OPAL. Well, ef you feel that way—

ROSIE. On the other han', if it wuz somethin' I could use an' ain't got, I wouldn't want to hurt yore feelin's by refusin'.

OPAL. I'll come up with somethin', dearie.

ROSIE. Jes so it ain't somethin' you don't hafta feed, peel or polish.

OPAL. You jes leave it to me, dearie. How old you gonna be this year, Rosie?

ROSIE. Same as las'.

OPAL. What wuz that?

ROSIE. Well, ef you want me to be *exact*, I'm still hoverin' between Hoover an' Carter.

OPAL. That's exact enough—that's somewhere this side of Medicare.

ROSIE. What about *you*?

OPAL. Forty-nine an' holdin'.

ROSIE. It's terrible how quick time goes by. Seems like only yesterday I had that little farm, some ducks an' a husban'.

OPAL. You still miss him, dearie?

ROSIE. No. But I shore miss them ducks. Remember the one that wuz a pet?

OPAL. Donald?

ROSIE. (*Nods.*) That sweet old duck jes' adored me. Followed me everywhere. That lousy husband of mine wanted to eat him. I wish I could on house-broke him.

OPAL. Who—the duck or yore husband?

ROSIE. An' when Donald got run over, I cried for two days.

OPAL. Rosie—you jes give me an' inspiration!

ROSIE. What about?

OPAL. Never min'. But yore in fer a nice surprise on your birthday. Jes' trus' me, dearie. (*Puts painting away.*)

ROSIE. Well, I dunno. Most of the surprises in my life, I coulda done without. Includin' my weddin' night.

OPAL. Would you take him back ef he wuz to show up, dearie? I mean your husband—not the duck.

7

ROSIE. That wuz fifteen years ago he ran off 'n left me. He's probably dead, too, now.

OPAL. Oh, then you wouldn't want him back.

ROSIE. I should have listened to my cards. They warned me he wuz no good.

OPAL. Well, you got to admit, Rosie, he *wuz* good lookin'. (*Adds.*) For a dwarf.

ROSIE. I don't want to talk about that dirty little over-sexed runt. Ef ever a man was sex-ridden—he wuz. (*Takes out her cards.*) Lets see ef the card got anything better fer you today. Fate an' the weather got one thing in common—they both change without warnin'.

OPAL. Oh, Rosie—las' time them cards said I was gonna come into a lot of money—an' it never happened.

ROSIE. The moon wasn't right. (*Lays out cards.*) Now let's see ef there's bin iny change fer the better. Put both your han's on the cards, dearie.

OPAL. Why?

ROSIE. That's to establish contact with the dead.

OPAL. You shore got a gift fer brightenin' up the mornin', Rosie.

ROSIE. Now say—abba—cadaba—cadaba.

OPAL. Why?

ROSIE. That's ghost talk.

OPAL. Abba—cadaba—cadaba.

ROSIE. Now we're in gear. Let's see what's in the cards. (*Puts a card down.*) Oh, Opal, oh!

OPAL. What's the matter—I'm in trouble already?

ROSIE. Look! (*Points to card.*) That's you. The Queen.

OPAL. Where? I don't see no Queen.

ROSIE. The King's on top of you—there.

OPAL. I'm a church goin' Baptist, dearie. You get that King off of me.

ROSIE. It jes mean he's got evil intentions.

OPAL. Rosie—I wasn't born yesterday. Ya don't need to explain what he's got on his min' if he's on top of me.

ROSIE. He's after somethin' different.

OPAL. He's too late.

ROSIE. (*Puts card down.*) Wait! Here come the Queen.

OPAL. An' high time.

ROSIE. Oh, Opal, somethin' don't smell right here.

OPAL. I got some cabbage cookin'.

8

ROSIE. You know what the Queen is sayin' to the King?

OPAL. Git up.

ROSIE. She's tellin' him to take somethin' away from you that's very valuable.

OPAL. At my age—it ain't valuable.

ROSIE. There's money in it, Opal.

OPAL. I know but I ain't the type.

ROSIE. (*Puts another card down.*) Wait—the Jack is on the King. That's gonna help you, Opal.

OPAL. Well, not from where I'm at.

ROSIE. Look—the Queen is on top of the Jack now.

OPAL. Sounds like one of them orgies I read about.

ROSIE. You don't understan'. The Jack means money. He's tryin' to he'p you.

OPAL. Well, money always he'ps but tell him to git that King off me and then we'll talk business.

ROSIE. Opal—look—yore saved! It's the Ace of Diamonds to the rescue. You're on top of the King, now!

OPAL. Rosie—you don't really believe that means anything, do you?

ROSIE. Why not? Does anybody know whin fate is goin' to come knockin' at yore door? Do they? (*There is a knock at the door.*) There—you see—someone is knockin' at yore door. Do you know who? Could be anybody.

OPAL. Jes so it ain't a ghost. (*Calls.*) Come in—it ain't locked. (*The door opens and a middle-age couple enter. The woman, "Queenie" Derwent, has faded blonde hair and is rather flamboyantly dressed with many bracelets. Her husband, "Desmond" Dolittle Derwent is equally theatrical in his attire. He carries himself regally with a jewelled cane.*)

DESMOND. Excuse me—but would I be mistaken in assuming that one of you ladies might be Opal Kronkie?

OPAL. Well, you'd insult my fren ef you thought *she* was. Come in!

ROSIE. I'm jes the pretty one.

DESMOND. (*Draws himself up proudly.*) I—am Desmond Dolittle Derwent. (*He waits expectantly.*) Do you happen to be aware of what that means?

OPAL. Shore. Yore Desmond Dolittle Derwent.

DESMOND. Evidently you do not attend the theater.

QUEENIE. (*Aside.*) Or read.

9

DESMOND. (*Proudly*.) We happen to be the stars of your local stock company this summer. We were told we might find some costumes here.

QUEENIE. Explain what we're looking for, King.

ROSIE. (*Rises*.) What'd you call him!

QUEENIE. King. Last year in Texas, he was voted King of Community Theater by *Turkey World*.

ROSIE. King! Didn't I tell you, Opal, the cards don't lie.

QUEENIE. What *is* she talking about?

OPAL. Nothin'. She et a bad oyster. She don't feel well.

DESMOND. (*Indicating his wife*.) And this talented lady is my wife, Queenie Derwent.

ROSIE. Queenie!

QUEENIE. Yes. Do you recognize me?

ROSIE. Only from the cards. Opal—send 'em away before it's too late. Them names is trouble fer you. The cards has warned you. Don't spit in the face of facts, Opal.

QUEENIE. What *is* she talking about?

OPAL. Now, Rosie dear, there lots of folks around called King or Queen.

QUEENIE. Yes—England, for instance.

ROSIE. Opal! Say aba—cadaba—cadaba! Quick.

OPAL. What fer!

ROSIE. It'll break the spell. You'll be saved from that bad smell around you.

DESMOND. Is she quite sane?

QUEENIE. Is she your mother?

ROSIE. Mother!

OPAL. It's jes she's upset. On top of that bad oyster, she had a bad dream. An' business has bin bad, too. So she ain't herself. She owns "Rosie's Hot Meat Ball Stan'" on the highway.

ROSIE. I also tell fortunes with my hot meat balls—costs you a quarter more, tho.

QUEENIE. I'll drop in some day—with my food stamps.

OPAL. So relax, Rosie. A lot of things in life jes happen to all look alike—eggs fer 'ninstance.

ROSIE. An' some of em is rotten.

OPAL. (*To Queenie*.) So yore play actors. I shoulda know'd that the minute I laid eyes on you.

QUEENIE. Indeed? Why?

OPAL. The *fur* yore wearing. I'll bet that's real muskrat.

QUEENIE. It happens to be mink.

OPAL. Well, I guess it takes one to know one. (*To Desmond.*) An' you. Them shoes. I know real leather whin I see it. That's gen-u-wine cowhide. Hers, too.

DESMOND. It happens to be alligator.

ROSIE. You shoot it yoreself?

OPAL. Oh, Rosie—you know better than that. Law don't allow it enymore. You wait 'till they die natural an' then you kin skin em for shoes.

ROSIE. Never heard of goin' *huntin'* fer dead alligators.

QUEENIE. I find the subject less than stimulating. Could we change it?

OPAL. Shore, why don't you set down, dearie, an' take a load off yore alligators. (*Almost pushes her into a rocker.*) You find that chair comfortable?

QUEENIE. Does anyone?

OPAL. Belonged to my Grandma Kronkie. She died in that chair, poor dear. Well now. You know I never met no real live round actors in the flesh before. But then, you mus' look different onstage.

QUEENIE. Did you see *Lear* last week?

OPAL. No—don't think I even know him. What does he do?

QUEENIE. *He* is a *play.* My husband—if I do say so myself— was superb! Your local paper said "incredible." And—"a performance you'll never forget!"

OPAL. Well, I don't read no newspapers until they're at least a year old. By that time, it's too late to git excited about the terrible things that's happined and whatever's bin did is did an' can't be undid. An' you sleep a lot better knowin' what you missed is better missed an' since you can't save the world enyhow, you might as well save yoreself worryin' about it. Ole news is bes' news.

QUEENIE. You must come to see *me,* next week. I'm playing— (*She lights a cigarette, exhales lustily.*) —"St. Joan."

ROSIE. Got any free tickets?

OPAL. Now, Rosie! Show business is a business like eny other business. An' it ain't good business to give business away. You don't give away yore meatballs—an' you don't see me givin' away enything here, do you?

ROSIE. Might be an improvement.

DESMOND. We were told we might find quite a few things here we could use in our future plays.

11

OPAL. Well. I got three floors here, all filled with interestin' things folks has thow'd away. An' the interestin' thing about things that's bin thro'd away, is that ef you save 'em long enough, they becomes antiques an' the same folk that thow'd 'em away, buys 'em back agin. Ef they live that long.

QUEENIE. What sort of things do you have?

OPAL. Everything from the Lord's Prayer on the head of a pin to a shrunken human head on a stick.

QUEENIE. (Aside.) Not a relative, I hope.

ROSIE. I'd take the pin, if I wuz you.

DESMOND. Well, actually what we're looking for is money.

ROSIE. (Leaps up.) I told you, Opal! I told you! Call the police.

DESMOND. I am referring to stage money. I was told that a local magician's widow gave you all her late husband's costumes along with a trunkful of stage money.

ROSIE. You never told me that, Opal. So you see—the cards was right after all. You came into money.

OPAL. It wuz jes' plain ole stage money, Rosie—you can't even paper the wall with it.

QUEENIE. Well, that's one thing we're looking for. You see, after St. Joan, King is doing Brewster's Millions.

DESMOND. We need quite a bit. How much of this stage money do you think you have?

OPAL. Oh, eight or ten million, I guess. You kin have the whole ten million for two bucks.

DESMOND. Two dollars?

OPAL. Well, that's includin' the trunk.

QUEENIE. We'll take it.

OPAL. But first, I got to see ef I kin find it. (Starts for the stairs.) While I'm gone why don't you folks look around an' see ef there's anything else you might need. It takes me a little time to remember where I put things so I won't forgit.

ROSIE. I'll be goin', Opal. An' you be careful. Remember what was in the cards.

OPAL. Well, thank you, sweetheart, fer comin' over an' fin'in' me alive.

ROSIE. Well, jes' stay that way. At least fer my birthday.

OPAL. I'll try, dearie. (To others.) You folks jes' make yoreselves at home.

QUEENIE. (Aside.) God forbid. (Opal goes out.)

ROSIE. Opel don't never throw nothin' away. Not even food.

Takes it in a bag when she goes scroungin'. Why, I seen her with as many as fifteen cats followin' her little wagon. Dogs, too.

QUEENIE. Too bad someone doesn't write a play about her.

ROSIE. I been thinkin' about doin' that myself. Writin' a play.

QUEENIE. Why not? Everyone else does.

ROSIE. Ef I did, I'd call it *Everybody Loves Opal*. Because that's the God's truth. She ain't got an enemy in the world. An' she jes' loves everybody.

QUEENIE. So you said—cats and dogs.

ROSIE. I wuz listenin's jest las' week to a feller on T.V. talkin' about play actors. He wuz tellin' about some famous actress named Sarah Bernhardt. You know her?

DESMOND. Sarah Bernhardt died before my wife was even conceived.

ROSIE. *That* long ago! Anyhow this feller said she wuz still actin' when she wuz seventy—an' with a wooden leg, too.

QUEENIE. An actor's talent is *not* in the legs.

ROSIE. Well, I shore wouldn't want to say that to Fred Astaire. (*She goes out.*)

DESMOND. Too bad we're not doing *Macbeth*. We could cast two of the witches right here.

QUEENIE. As long as we're waiting—we might as well see if we can find anything we might be able to use. (*They start taking articles out of barrels and boxes.*) I could use some fake jewelry.

DESMOND. Well, dear—I've found *just* the thing for you. (*Holds it up.*) Here's a charming necklace made of acorns.

QUEENIE. Those aren't acorns, dear. They look more like teeth.

DESMOND. Human?

QUEENIE. It wouldn't surprise me. Get rid of them.

DESMOND. (*Holds up a dress.*) Now. Look at this horror. Can you imagine anyone being caught dead in a dress like this?

QUEENIE. Yes—a retarded Chinese female impersonator. (*Holds up cape.*) This must be the cape that magician wore.

DESMOND. Too bad we're not playing *Dracula* for these dumb audiences here.

QUEENIE. What makes you think we're not.

DESMOND. Here's a Spanish comb. That might come in handy for stabbing someone.

QUEENIE. Or serving spaghetti.

DESMOND. What do you suppose is in this chest?

QUEENIE. Probably a mummy. Don't open it.

13

DESMOND. Look—she's got a box of sheets. Now, what home do you suppose *they* came from.

QUEENIE. Oh, some funeral home.

DESMOND. And here's a feather boa. Aren't they supposed to make a woman look sexy?

QUEENIE. Only if she's nude. (*Finds Opal's painting.*) Will you look at this monstrosity? (*Holds up picture.*) Now, who'd ever buy a picture of a dead duck and a rotten apple?

DESMOND. Oh, a butcher shop—to hang in the window.

QUEENIE. There's only one other place I'd hang it and you know where. (*Throws it aside.*)

DESMOND. (*Holds up muff.*) What in God's name is *this!*

QUEENIE. It's a muff, stupid.

DESMOND. What's it used for?

QUEENIE. To keep biscuits hot, dear.

DESMOND. I don't think there is anything here we want. You look if you want to. I'll read my paper. (*Sits at table and takes paper out of his pocket.*)

QUEENIE. Do you suppose she has any wigs? I can always use wigs.

DESMOND. (*Reading paper.*) No—but I'm sure she has a few scalps here.

QUEENIE. (*Takes out a teddy bear.*) Now—here's something we might use if we do *The Curious Savage.*

DESMOND. The what?

QUEENIE. Oh, you know—that Patrick play that was such a flop on Broadway, with Lillian Gish. She had a teddy bear filled with all her money.

DESMOND. I didn't see it.

QUEENIE. You had to be quick. But Lillian Gish was so lovely. Wore a blue wig and—

DESMOND. Wait. (*Leaps to his feet.*) Did you see this!

QUEENIE. See what?

DESMOND. Oh, my God—I can't believe it.

QUEENIE. What is it!—Don't tell me the theater burned down!

DESMOND. Listen. (*Reads.*) "Valuable Dutch Masterpiece Missing from Hockerheimer Museum."

QUEENIE. So what. You frightened me.

DESMOND. Wait. (*Reads on.*) "The famous painting, *Mallard and Apple,* by the Dutch Renaissance artist Van Von Vanderdam, valued at one million dollars, was discovered missing today by the board of trustees."

14

QUEENIE. You think that picture—
DESMOND. Get it! See if it's signed.
QUEENIE. (*Gets canvas and unrolls it. Then reads.*) Van Von Vanderdam!
DESMOND. It's the same picture!
QUEENIE. And she has that Vanderdam here.
DESMOND. Damn!
QUEENIE. But how'd *she* get it. Do you think she stole it?
DESMOND. Not a chance. Listen. (*Reads.*) "This valuable painting had been removed several weeks ago for cleaning and placed in a store room at the rear of the museum. It is feared that new workmen engaged to enlarge this area threw this priceless masterpiece into their rubbish under the impression it was a piece of discarded canvas."
QUEENIE. And that goony bird *found* it!
DESMOND. But listen to this! (*Reads.*) "The insurance company is offering a reward of fifty thousand dollars to anyone who finds this valuable canvas and returns it to the Museum."
QUEENIE. Fifty thousand. Do you think she knows?
DESMOND. No—but *we* do. We'll make a deal with her.
QUEENIE. She said herself she doesn't read the papers.
DESMOND. We'll tell her about it and make her promise to share the reward.
QUEENIE. Are you crazy? We'll buy it and keep the reward ourselves.
DESMOND. Of course. If we pay her what she asks, it'll be an honest deal.
QUEENIE. What'll we offer her? Two dollars?
DESMOND. Make it five. She might get suspicious. Fifty thousand dollars! We can have our mortgage lifted.
QUEENIE. And I can have my face lifted.
DESMOND. And we could collect our unemployment insurance in a Rolls-Royce.
QUEENIE. We've got to be very tricky how we trick her, dear.
DESMOND. We're actors, aren't we?
QUEENIE. We'll have to pretend we are interested in some of her other things first and *then* decided to buy the painting as a kind of gag.
DESMOND. She might even give it to us if we buy enough things first.
QUEENIE. Give her some tickets to see our show and then she might just give us the painting out of gratitude.

DESMOND. In case we have to pay cash, how much have you got with you?

QUEENIE. (*Looks in her purse.*) Five dollars and two airmail stamps.

DESMOND. (*Reaches into his pocket.*) I've got thirty dollars and a subway token.

QUEENIE. That's a fortune to her.

DESMOND. Do you think she'd take our check if we had to go higher?

QUEENIE. Why not—we look honest, don't we?

DESMOND. Be careful! She's coming back. *Smile.*

OPAL. (*Comes down carrying a small trunk.*) Well, I finally remembered where I'd forgot I put it. Sorry I took so long but I had to empty a couple of rat traps first.

QUEENIE. Oh, we haven't minded waiting at all. You have so many lovely things, we're tempted to buy them all.

DESMOND. Where do you ever find such rare objects? Every item is a treasure.

OPAL. Well, if I do say so myself, I got taste. When you ain't got looks—taste is the next best thing next to cash.

QUEENIE. And what you've *done* to this room! It could start a trend. Crude is so chic nowadays. And basic is so honest.

OPAL. Well, now ain't you nice to say that. (*Puts trunk on table and opens it.*) Here's that stage money you wanted. About ten million, I was told. You wanna count it?

DESMOND. What's a million more or less between friends, Opal? We trust you.

OPAL. Jes doa'n try to spend it. You might get rooked.

DESMOND. I believe you said two dollars?

OPAL. Ef that ain't too much?

DESMOND. For ten million? *And* the trunk? (*Hands her money.*) You can spend *that*—it's real.

QUEENIE. Like us.

OPAL. You don't need to tell me that, Mister. A nice gentleman like you wouldn't have no counterfeits. You see, I got a lucky gift— I know when to trust someone.

DESMOND. Oh, you're so right, madam. No matter how good an actor may be there're two things he can't hide—love—and greed.

OPAL. An' I jes know yore a good actor. It shows all over you. I kin tell.

DESMOND. Why don't you come and see us perform, Opal? (*Hands her a ticket.*) Here's a ticket for our next show. A gift from *us* to *you.* Free.

OPAL. Well, ain't you nice. What's yore play called?

DESMOND. *You Can't Take It With You.*

QUEENIE. Opal, dear—may I call you dear? I feel as if we're old friends already.

OPAL. Well, I try to feel that way about *everbody.* It's a good start an' saves time.

QUEENIE. Well, Opal dear, there are so many things I want to buy from you but I don't want to rob you of *all* your treasures.

OPAL. Well, I'd be selfish, hoardin' all my goodies jes for myself alone.

QUEENIE. For instance—this *fabulous* necklace—so—so *of* today. What are the stones, dear?

OPAL. Gall stones. Used to belong to a doctor's wife.

QUEENIE. Gall stones!

OPAL. Yep. Each one of them stones come from somebody famous. Senators—movie stars—a Navajo chief—and at least two Democrats.

QUEENIE. No Republicans?

OPAL. No—I guess they keep their stones. Anyhow there ain't another necklace like this in the world.

QUEENIE. I can well believe you. Could you bear to part with it?

OPAL. Well, I *wuz* askin' three bucks fer it but seein' as you like it so much—you kin have it fer two. (*Hands her the necklace.*)

QUEENIE. (*Passes it to Desmond.*) Here dear—I've just bought a fabulous conversation piece.

DESMOND. What about this feather boa, dear? Couldn't you use that for some special occasion?

QUEENIE. How could I live without it? It's so—so *in.*

OPAL. Try it on, dearie. (*Drapes it around her neck.*) There now—don't she look like a real queen! Wait a minute—I got jes the thing to go with it. Close yore eyese, dearie. (*Reaches into a barrel and takes out a large picture hat with trailing ribbons. She puts it on Queenie's head.*) There now. Ain't that a picture?

QUEENIE. (*Reaches out from under the hat.*) Where is everybody?

DESMOND. It's very—you—dear.

OPAL. Makes her look ten years younger, don't it.

DESMOND. (*Laughs.*) It should. No one can see her under it.

17

OPAL. Only one thing's missin'. I know! (*She grabs the muff and hands it to Queenie.*) Put yore han's in this and yore Mrs. Rockefeller in person. (*Queenie puts her hand in the muff and screams.*)

DESMOND. What is it!

QUEENIE. There's a mouse in it! (*Drops it on floor.*)

OPAL. Lemme see. (*Shakes muff. Queenie moves away. Something drops out.*) It's jes the ear muffs. I *wonderin'* where I'd put 'em, I'll throw them in free with the muff.

DESMOND. How much for the lot? (*Queenie hands him hat and boa.*)

OPAL. Four bucks sound fair to you?

DESMOND. Make it five. We wouldn't want to rob you. See anything else, dear?

QUEENIE. Let me look. There's so much. (*Picks up canvas and unrolls it.*) Oh, look dear. Isn't this quaint? (*To Opal.*) Did you paint this yourself?

OPAL. Lord, I couldn't paint the side of a barn. No—somebody throw'd it away an' I picked it up.

DESMOND. Where?

OPAL. Oh, in the alley jes off Pussywillow an' Coolidge.

DESMOND. You mean behind the museum?

OPAL. That's right—there was a lot of rubbish—plaster an' stuff.

QUEENIE. It's rather interesting, isn't it—for a primitive painter.

DESMOND. Yes—but we've no use for it, dear.

QUEENIE. Wait! Do you know what just occurred to me?

DESMOND. Lunch?

QUEENIE. Well, you *know*, stupid! (*Jabs him with her elbow. Turns to Opal.*) Do you know Ibsen's *Wild Duck?*

OPAL. Didn't even know he had one.

DESMOND. Oh, yes—of course. *The Wild Duck.* Ibsen.

QUEENIE. It's our final production. I'm to play the lead.

OPAL. Yore gonna play a dead duck?

QUEENIE. And think how *perfect* this picture would be on the wall of our set. So symbolic.

DESMOND. Very.

QUEENIE. We'll take this one, too, Opal. And we'll see that you have seats opening night.

OPAL. Well now, I'm mighty sorry to tell you but that's the only thing here that ain't for sale.

DESMOND. What do you mean—ain't for—isn't for sale!

OPAL. Well, you see—I'm savin' it fer a birthday present.

QUEENIE. Oh, well, you could substitute something else, couldn't you?

OPAL. Not in this case. It's got a special meaning.

DESMOND. We'll give you ten dollars for it.

OPAL. But it ain't worth *two* dollars.

DESMOND. It doesn't make any difference. We happen to be perfectionists. It will help establish the mood of the play.

QUEENIE. Don't be so frugal, dear. (*To Opal.*) I'll tell you what we'll do because we like you so. We'll give you fifteen.

OPAL. Why, I'd be robbin' you.

DESMOND. You'd be doing us a favor. And Ibsen.

OPAL. Why I couldn't sleep nights knowin' I sold my conscience for fifteen dollars.

QUEENIE. We'll make it twenty to help your conscience feel better.

OPAL. But you could go to any butcher shop and get a real dead duck for a buck an' a half.

QUEENIE. A real dead duck hanging on the wall of our set would be distracting, Opal, dear. Twenty-five.

OPAL. Folks—don't think I'm greedy but this here picture is gonna bring happiness to my bes fren and I'd be sellin' her happiness for twenty-five dollars. An' I couldn't do that.

DESMOND. Thirty.

OPAL. No but I'll tell you what I will do. I happen to have a stuffed penguin upstairs you can have for fifty cents.

QUEENIE. We don't want a penguin.

OPAL. A hoot owl maybe?

QUEENIE. We want the *picture*. Nothing else will do.

DESMOND. Who is this person you're saving the picture for? Maybe I could persuade her.

OPAL. No—that's jes what I don't want. I wanna surprise this fren.

QUEENIE. Besides—time is running out.

DESMOND. Alright. Forty dollars and that's as high as we'll go. It's your last chance, Opal.

OPAL. This don't make sense.

DESMOND. Forty-five.

OPAL. Mister—it ain't that I'm stubborn. But I happen to love this fren of mine. And I can't put no price on love. I'd feel like Judas.

DESMOND. Judas only got thirty pieces—we're offering you forty-five.

QUEENIE. Fifty.

OPAL. It ain't the money. You could offer me a hun'erd and I still wouldn't take it.

DESMOND. All right— a hundred.

OPAL. I got a feelin' one of us is crazy.

DESMOND. You're refusing a hundred dollars for a picture not worth two. Does that answer your question who's crazy.

QUEENIE. We're offering you that much because it's worth it to the success of our play.

OPAL. No you ain't. An' you ain't bein' truthful with me neither.

QUEENIE. What do you mean?

OPAL. I know I look like a fool but I ain't, really. Because I know why yore offering that much money.

DESMOND. You do?

OPAL. Yes, sir. Charity. You feel sorry for me and wanna help. I know I look like I ain't got nothin' more 'n a zip code but even ef I wuz starvin' I would accept no charity. So God bless you both. Yore good people. An' I thank you. (Kisses Queenie.)

QUEENIE. Opal, I swear I don't feel sorry for you.

DESMOND. Do you have a Bible?

OPAL. Ef I wuz to sell this here duck at all, I couldn't take more 'n two dollars because that's all it's worth. An' I don't cheat no one.

DESMOND. We'll give you two dollars, then.

OPAL. Nope. It ain't fer sale. (Holds up dress.) How about this here dress? Long skirts draggin' on the ground is comin' back in style.

DESMOND. We'll take it. (Throws it in trunk.) Opal, accept the hundred dollars and buy your friend some live little baby ducks instead.

QUEENIE. Yes! Just think how happy a hundred ittsy bitty baby ducks would make her. Maybe two hundred—little yellow ducklings.

OPAL. Nope. City won't let her keep no ducks. How about this here feather fan? Real gen-u-wine peacock tail feathers. You don't see many of these anymore.

DESMOND. We'll take it. (Grabs it and throws it in trunk.) I'll tell you what I'm going to do, Opal. My dear wife has her heart set on that picture. And she also happens to have a weak heart. I have to be careful not to upset her. So I'm going to offer you two hundred—for the sake of my dear wife and her weak heart.

OPAL. Oh, you got a weak heart, dearie. My Gramma Kronkie had the same thing. Left lots of medicine here whin she died. (*Gets bottles.*) This here kept her alive till a hundred an' five. I must have a whole case full left over. Here.

DESMOND. We'll take it. Now, will you take the two hundred from us?

OPAL. Nope.

DESMOND. Three hundred?

OPAL. Nope.

DESMOND. Four hundred?

OPAL. Nope.

DESMOND. Five hundred!

QUEENIE. Oh-h-h. Oh—this is getting too much for my heart. (*She clutches her heart.*) Oh—

DESMOND. Queenie—what is it! Are you going to faint? (*She staggers back into a chair. It collapses and Queenie falls with it.*) Darling—are you hurt?

QUEENIE. Of course I'm hurt, you fool.

OPAL. Hold her mouth open. I'll give her some of this here medicine. (*Holds up bottle.*)

QUEENIE. Help me up—you idiot. Never mind that poison.

DESMOND. You see, Opal— You almost killed her.

OPAL. Sorry about that chair, dearie. I glued that leg back on an' coulda swore it woulda held an elephant. How about *yore* leg.

QUEENIE. I may never walk again.

OPAL. Well, now, I jes happen to have a slightly used pair of crutches. You can have one fer a quarter or get a bargain at a dollar a pair.

QUEENIE. Desmond—take me out of here before I start screaming!

OPAL. Oh, dear—does it hurt that bad, dearie?

DESMOND. Sweetheart—we can't leave. We haven't got that—

QUEENIE. I know what I'm doing. There is more than one way to skin a cat.

OPAL. You skin yore knee, too, dearie?

DESMOND. Are you sure— ?

QUEENIE. Trust me—I'll explain later. There's still tomorrow. (*She starts limping to the door.*)

DESMOND. I hope you know what you're doing.

QUEENIE. I do. It's going to be all right.

OPAL. I shore hope so. I shoulda warned you not to sit in that chair. Gramma Kronkie died in it. They don't make chairs like

21

them enymore. Or people neither. (*They go out without speaking.*) I hope you ain't mad. (*Waits a minute. Calls after them.*) Hey Mister—you forgot all yore goodies you paid for. You coming back tomorrow to git 'em? (*Desmond races back in—past the trunk and grabs up the newspaper he left behind. And races out again.*) Now, that's what I like to see. A man so worried about his wife he forgits all about a trunkful of money—even if it is only paper. An' that's because *he's* a real hisself—a *real* gen-u-wine gentleman. An' you don't see many of them enymore neither.

CURTAIN

ACT TWO

PLACE: *The same.*

TIME: *The next day.*

AT RISE: *Opal is sitting at her table finishing her tea and humming to herself. She rises to take cup back to alcove where she dips it in a bucket and hangs it up.*

OPAL. Well—time's awastin'. I better wrap Rosie's birthday gift. She's gonna be forty-eight again before you know it. (*Brings canvas and birthday wrapping paper to table. She unties the rope around the picture and looks at it again.*) I still kain't un'erstan' why enyone would wanna paint a dead duck ef they could paint a live naked woman like mos' artists. Still an' all, I'm glad this here artist had a duck 'cause— (*She starts wrapping gift.*) Rosie is jes gonna love this here "pitchure." Breaks her heart she ain't allowed to raise ducks now she's in the city limits. You kin raise delinquents but no ducks. Well, this here will remind her of whin she lived in the country. That pet of hers—Donald—she loved that duck more'n her husband. Kain't say I blame her neither— they wuz both about the same size. Only that dwarf she married couldn't even lay an egg. Laid everything else, tho. Makes you wonder sometimes what yore married fren's see in each other. But thin, they always wonder themselves after the divorce. Jes' goes to prove that love ain't blind—it's jes' nearsighted, cross-eyed and color blind. (*Finishes wrapping present.*) Now sompin' real pretty to tie it up with. (*Looks around.*) I know. (*Gets ribboned hat.*) That nice play actress ain't gonna miss one ribbon. (*Cuts ribbon.*) Red. That's kinda Italian. (*Ties up gift.*) Now, ain't that pretty? Ef you had some whipped cream you could eat it. An' that there wrappin' paper! Sometimes, nowadays the paper costs more'n the present. Speakin' of paper, where'd I put that roll of wallpaper I bin savin'. (*Looks around.*) I remember. (*Takes a roll of wallpaper from a barrel.*) Now if I'd only remembered this here wallpaper, I coulda saved a buck an' a half. (*She takes the discarded rope from the canvas and ties up the roll of wallpaper with it.*) Agrivatin' to realize where you coulda saved money whin it's too late. Like missin' a bus an' it rains. (*Puts wallpaper behind*

23

cabinet in alcove.) But *enything* that's too late is agravatin'. 'Specially a fire truck. (*Returns to table.*) Well, I'll jes' take Rosie's dead duck upstairs an' put it somewhere's where I'll remember ef I don't forgit. (*She starts up the stairs. Halfway, she turns around, backs up the rest of the way.*) When you got a lot of steps to climb, its always a good idear to back up some of 'em. Exercises both sides of yore legs. (*A few moments after she has disappeared, there is a knock at the door. When there is no answer, Desmond and his wife enter. She is carrying a bouquet of flowers —and limps slightly.*)

DESMOND. Miss Kronkie?

QUEENIE. Opal? She's probably upstairs.

DESMOND. What do you suppose she's doing?

QUEENIE. Peeling lizards.

DESMOND. Now don't get caustic. We have a plan to follow out. (*Calls upstairs.*) Miss Kronkie?

OPAL. (*Offstage.*) Who is it?

DESMOND. Us. Your friends from the theater.

OPAL. Who?

QUEENIE. The thespians.

OPAL. (*Offstage.*) Oh. Well, make yourselves a cup of tea. Sugar's in a tin can marked moth balls. I'll be right down. Hep' yourselves.

QUEENIE. Tea! I'd just as soon drink bat milk.

DESMOND. Where do you suppose the picture is?

QUEENIE. Oh, probably buried in the basement with several corpses.

DESMOND. Now, don't be pessimistic dear. We have a foolproof plan.

QUEENIE. At least we've got a plan and we've certainly got the fool.

DESMOND. And it's going to work.

QUEENIE. Do you know how many drops to use? After all—we don't want to risk killing her—not for fifty thousand.

DESMOND. The reward has been raised to seventy-five.

QUEENIE. Oh, well that's different.

DESMOND. And my cousin told me just how many drops will knock her out. Remember—he used to be a bartender.

QUEENIE. If it works—we'll buy him a bloody mary.

DESMOND. The hard part will be to convince her that we really want to make an actress of her.

24

QUEENIE. That's the easiest part. *Everbody* thinks they can act. Even actresses.

DESMOND. Once we've tricked her into thinking she could be an actress—we'll have to act out Juliet's death scene where she has to take poison. I'll put some drops in her tea and knock her out while we search for the Van Von Vanderdam.

QUEENIE. It sounds simple. I only hope she falls for it.

DESMOND. Quiet—she's coming back. (*Changes attitude.*) Do you think I had on too much makeup last night?

QUEENIE. It doesn't matter, dear, when I'm onstage. (*Picks up garment.*) Oh, look—a corset! I haven't seen one of these since I was weaned. (*Opal comes down stairs and stops halfway.*)

OPAL. What was that you jes' called yoreselves?

DESMOND. Thespians. Quite often we're referred to as— thespians.

OPAL. (*Continues down.*) Oh, well, I wouldn't let that bother me none. You know how people talk.

QUEENIE. Opal, dear—we're *so* glad to see you again. (*Kisses her.*) You've done something to your hair, haven't you?

OPAL. No. Jes' combed it. How's yore ankle?

QUEENIE. Oh, it only hurts when I walk on it. Look—I've brought you some posies.

OPAL. Look like tulips to me.

QUEENIE. They are. I hope you like them.

OPAL. Why they ain't plastic neither!

QUEENIE. Of course not. We wouldn't want anything false in *our* friendship.

OPAL. Why we ain't had real flowers in here since Hoover was President. That's whin Grandma Kronkie died. Well, I shore do thank you.

DESMOND. And *I've* a little token of our esteem for you, too. (*Hands her package.*)

OPAL. Why that paper alone musta set you back a buck or two.

DESMOND. What is money between friends?

OPAL. Trouble, sometimes. Unless they don't care about it. And they's very few of them left. (*Opens package.*) Well, whadda you know—a water pitcher for the flowers.

QUEENIE. It's a vase for the flowers. (*She pronounces it "vahz."*)

OPAL. Vahz?

QUEENIE. When its pure crystal—it's "vahz."

OPAL. Well how about that! Pure crystal.

QUEENIE. Like you, Opal. Without a flaw.

OPAL. Well, now—yore jes' two of the nicest people I ever met.

DESMOND. Oh, there's a lot like us.

OPAL. An' I jes' wish I could hug 'em all.

QUEENIE. Oh, by the way, Opal, what did you do with that duck picture?

OPAL. Oh, I put it away where I wouldn't forget it. It ain't that I forget that's agravatin'! It's that I forgit what I fergot.

QUEENIE. You know, Opal, we've been thinking about you constantly. Someone like you, who's such a unique character, really belongs in the theater. I've never seen a face with so much character.

OPAL. Well, whin yore born ugly, character is about all you got goin' fer you. Unless you got money. Want some tea? (*Makes tea.*)

QUEENIE. Thank you, no—I've just had hiccups. One reason we're back so early is we've come up with a brilliant idea for you.

OPAL. How about some broken cookies? Baker fren' of mine Angelo Fettucini down on Pussywillow and Cattail Road lets me have a whole bag of broken cookies fer a dime. Won'erful feller. Real gen-u-wine. Italian.

DESMOND. We're dieting. Now, we hope you'll agree to what we ourselves have decided will be a great opportunity for you.

OPAL. Poor Angelo had a terrible tragedy. Lost his wife on a bus. Turned out it turned over. In a blizzard. Whin they dug her out she was froze stiff. They propped her up against a tree until they could notify Angelo—that's Italian for Angel—an' tell him what had happened. He wuz bakin' raisin cookies whin they got him on the phone. Left his cookies an' wint on snowshoes to git her.

DESMOND. So we've come up with a plan for you.

QUEENIE. That may change your whole future, dear.

OPAL. Well, sir, whin poor Mr. Fettucini got to the scene of the accident an' seen his poor froze wife leanin' against a tree an' glarin' at him—he took it real bad.

QUEENIE. We want you to take our offer seriously, dear.

OPAL. Took off an' took to drink. Took a boat to Italy. Took him a year to git over his froze wife. Then one day he seen a lovely Italian belly dancer shakin' herself on the beach to git dry. Turned him to butter. Got sunburned watchin' her.

DESMOND. Have you ever thought about a career that could make you famous?

26

OPAL. Well, sir—they got married. They come back to his bakery on Pussywillow and Cattail Road an' started bakin raisin cookies again an' raisin' a family. Love opened his oven. She's happy as a loon jes' being Mrs. Angelo Quovadis Philomena Fettucini. But all that don't fit on her credit card. An' him—put on two helpers an' forty pounds. Won'erful feller. Real gen-u-wine. Bald-headed.
DESMOND. Opal. I want you to take yourself seriously for a moment.
OPAL. Well, I ain't sure that's a good idear. Only time it's time to take yoreself seriously is when yore sick. If you ain't sick an' take yoreself seriously—then yore sick.
DESMOND. Opal—have you ever considered acting?
OPAL. Do it every day. You see somebody that's maybe done you dirt an' you say "nice to see you." Or somebody that said a mean thing about you—you say "Have a nice day." That's actin'.
QUEENIE. No—that's manners. We mean on the stage.
OPAL. You mean a play-actor—like you? Fer money?
QUEENIE. For your fulfillment.
DESMOND. Have you ever been in a play?
OPAL. Once.
DESMOND. When was that?
OPAL. Well, I wuz in the second grade. Never got to third.
DESMOND. What did you play?
OPAL. A tree.
QUEENIE. A tree?
OPAL. Well, I started out as a butterfly but I didn't flit to suit the teacher so she made me a tree.
QUEENIE. I'm sure you gave a good solid performance.
OPAL. Teacher didn't think so. Whin the good fairy was dying, I had to scratch my nose.
QUEENIE. Well, King and I have decided you have all the qualities of a professional.
OPAL. A professional what?
DESMOND. Character actress. How would you like to join our company?
OPAL. Fer dinner?
DESMOND. As an actress. As my wife's understudy.
OPAL. Oh, I wouldn't be no good as a play actress! I ain't even a good cook.
QUEENIE. We think you're a wonderful type.
DESMOND. Have you seen many plays?

27

OPAL. I seen *Romeo an' Juliet* once. In the park. It wuz free. Started rainin'. Everbody lift but me. An' the actors. I rekon I'm the only one knows how it ended. 'Cept the actors.

DESMOND. *Romeo and Juliet.* Now isn't that a coincidence! That's the very play we've brought with us to have you read.

QUEENIE. Audition—you know.

OPAL. No, I don't know. What does that mean?

QUEENIE. Oh, take a scene at random and read it for us.

OPAL. Out loud?

QUEENIE. Just to see if you can project.

OPAL. Project what?

QUEENIE. Your voice. We'd like to determine how far you can be heard.

OPAL. Two miles. I won a hog-callin' contest when I wuz fifteen. Would that be far enough?

QUEENIE. If we played a stadium.

DESMOND. (*Hands her book.*) Here—I've picked out the death scene. See what you can do with it, Opal.

OPAL. Oh, I'd jes' be wastin' yore time. Besides, I'm too old.

QUEENIE. Was Bernhardt too old—at seventy?

DESMOND. With one leg.

QUEENIE. She'd turn over in her grave to hear you say that.

OPAL. Well, I wouldn't want to cause her no discomfort so ef you really want me to jes' try—

DESMOND. We want to see your name up there in lights. "Opal Kronkie." With a line up at the box office.

OPAL. Gittin' their money back.

QUEENIE. (*Opens book.*) Here, why don't you just read this part and we'll prompt you.

DESMOND. What can you lose?

OPAL. My sense of humor.

QUEENIE. (*Points to page.*) Start there.

OPAL. (*After a long wait.*) Which one am I? Romeo or Juliet?

QUEENIE. Juliet, of course. What else could you play?

OPAL. A tree.

QUEENIE. Go ahead. Begin.

OPAL. It says here this Juliet is sixteen.

DESMOND. We're going to play her a little older.

QUEENIE. Start anytime. (*Opal takes the book and tries to focus on it—close and then at arm's length.*) What are you doing?

OPAL. Guess I need my glasses. Ef I hold it too far away all I

see is black bugs an' if I hold it too close, my fingernail looks too big. (*Goes to a drawer and selects several pair.*) These ain't really mine. Minister's wife died—lovely woman—real gen-u-wine—and the preacher gimme all her glasses. Poor woman had St. Vitus Dance an' couldn't keep her teeth in—
QUEENIE. Opal—please—we have a matinee.
OPAL. (*Selects pair.*) I reckon I can read with these. One glass is missin'. I'll squint. (*Comes back* D.C.) Poor woman died in a elevator. Tenth floor. Jes' come from the dentist.
QUEENIE. Please start. We're waiting.
OPAL. (*Closes one eye.*) I can see now—ef I don't wiggle. (*She is silent a moment.*) Do I read all this!
QUEENIE. No, we'll skip down to the speech just before you take the poison, dear. Start here.
OPAL. (*Clears her throat.*) Do I stand or sit?
QUEENIE. Either one.
OPAL. I'll stan'. I jes' glued that chair together an' I don't think it's set yit.
QUEENIE. Do anything you want, Opal, and when you drink the love potion and start to pass out—we'll put you on the table. *Start.*
OPAL. Here?
QUEENIE. There.
OPAL. (*Straightens and clears throat. She bellows out.*) Oh, look!
QUEENIE. Opal—you're not calling pigs. Modulate.
OPAL. That means softer?
QUEENIE. Softer.
OPAL. Oh, look. Methinks— (*Turns to Queenie.*) Is that right? *Me* think?
QUEENIE. It's Shakespeare.
OPAL. Sounds Puerto Rican.
QUEENIE. *Please* go on.
OPAL. (*Reads.*) "Methinks I see. My cousin's ghost seeking. (*Takes deep breath.*) Out Romeo. That did split his body upon a—a—"
QUEENIE. Rapier.
OPAL. "—rapier's point." (*Then as if issuing an invitation.*) "Stay, Tybalt—" (*She pronounces it "Tie-balt."*)
QUEENIE. Tybalt.
OPAL. "Stay, Tybalt—stay. Romeo? I come. This do I drink to thee." (*Looks up.*) Thin I drink somethin'?
QUEENIE. Yes. Desmond will hand you a love potion that will

29

put you to sleep and you fall on a sarcophagus. (*Behind her, Desmond can be seen putting drops in a cup.*)

OPAL. A who?

QUEENIE. A kind of coffin. The table will do.

OPAL. How'm I doin' so far?

QUEENIE. I can truthfully say—you've sent chills down my spine.

OPAL. Gits easy whin you git into it, don't it?

DESMOND. (*Hands her cup.*) Here. Now you drink this to fool Romeo. It puts you to sleep.

OPAL. How long?

DESMOND. 'Till Romeo finds you and thinks you are dead. I'll be Romeo. You stay asleep and when I wake you, we play the rest of the scene. Go back to "Romeo, I come"—then take the drink—finish your line and fall on the table.

OPAL. (*Takes cup.*) Here?

QUEENIE. There.

OPAL. "Romeo—I come. This do I drink to thee." (*She downs the liquid.*)

QUEENIE. Beautiful! (*But Opal acts. She staggers about the stage, taking more time than Tristan to die. She starts to collapse on the floor.*)

DESMOND. No—no! On your sarcophagus. (*They lead her to the table and help her collapse.*)

QUEENIE. An Academy performance if ever I saw one.

DESMOND. Don't talk—don't break the mood—it's too perfect. Get a sheet.

OPAL. (*Sits up.*) There's sheets in that tin cracker box. (*Queenie gets sheet.*)

DESMOND. Now, you pretend to be drugged until I search for you and finally find you—still sleeping.

QUEENIE. (*Covers Opal.*) Then King kills himself and dies on top of you.

OPAL. (*Sits up.*) On top of me?

QUEENIE. It's in the play.

OPAL. It's in the cards according to Rosie. Shore hope she don't come in. She'd faint dead away. (*Covers head again.*)

DESMOND. Sleep, Juliet—sleep.

OPAL. (*Sits up.*) This gonna take long? I gotta put on my pot roast.

DESMOND. Not long. We just want to see how convincing you'll be when you waken and discover Romeo dead on top of you. (*Waits.*) Are you asleep, Opal? (*Waits. Opal snores.*)

QUEENIE. (*Whispers.*) How much did you give her?
DESMOND. (*Whispers.*) Just enough to give me time to find the picture. (*To Opal.*) Opal—can you hear me? (*There is a snore.*)
QUEENIE. Opal—the house is on fire.
DESMOND. She's out. It's safe.
QUEENIE. Where do you think she put it?
DESMOND. Who knows! We'll look upstairs first. (*They race up the stairs. There is a wait—then a knock on the door. Rosie enters.*)
ROSIE. I jes' come over to tell you I done your fortune again an' yore in fer a surprise. The Jack of Spades— (*She stops as she sees the "corpse" on the table.*) Oh! Oh—no! (*Races to the table. She lifts the sheet and screams.*) Oh, Opal—the cards wuz right. Gone! Gone forever! My only fren'. (*She staggers* c.*, falls to her knees, hands clasped, she closes her eyes and starts singing.*)
    "Rock of Ages
    Cleft for me
    Let me hide
    Myself in thee
(*Then louder.*)
    Let the water
    An' the blood
    From thy river
    Side which flowed
(*Behind her, Opal rises still covered by the sheet, Rosie, louder.*)
    Be of sin
    The double cure
    Cleanse me from
    Its quest and power"
OPAL. That you, Rosie? (*Rosie turns and sees Opal's apparent ghost. She crawls rapidly away.*)
ROSIE. No—no. Don't come git me, Opal. I ain't ready. I wuz yore fren'—remember? No, Opal—not me. I ain't paid my water bill. (*As Opal moves toward her, she faints. Opal takes off the sheet.*)
OPAL. What's the matter with you, Rosie? I ain't dead. Look at me. (*Kneels beside her.*) Feel me. Oh, Judas—she fainted. (*She takes the vase of flowers and hurls water and flowers on her. Rosie sputters and sits up. She starts to crawl away again.*)
ROSIE. No! No! Please don't lay a han' on me. I wuz yore fren'. I lover you, Opal. I brought you my meatballs.
OPAL. Rosie, will you believe me. I *ain't* dead. I wuz play-actin'.
ROSIE. You mean—pretendin'?

31

OPAL. Shore. Them two actors that wuz here yestidy ast me to— (*Looks around.*) Now where is he?

ROSIE. Who?

OPAL. Romeo. (*At this point Desmond and Queenie race down the stairs.*)

DESMOND. What's happened?

QUEENIE. We heard someone singing.

ROSIE. *I* wuz singin'. Got eny objections?

OPAL. What wuz you doin' upstairs?

QUEENIE. We—we were looking for the bathroom.

DESMOND. You—we had to go to the bathroom.

OPAL. Together?

DESMOND. What's she doing on the floor?

ROSIE. (*Angrily.*) I alwuz set on the floor! I'm part Indian.

DESMOND. (*To Opal.*) How did you wake up? You were supposed to be sleeping.

OPAL. Rosie's singing would raise the dead.

ROSIE. Well, are you goin' to leave me here on the floor settin' in water?

OPAL. (*Helps her up.*) Here—sweetheart—take my han'—it won't lead you to hell. Besides, yore settin' on my tulips.

ROSIE. Well, I mus' say yore some fren', Opal—pretendin' to be dead jes to scare the wits outta me.

OPAL. Now Rosie Montefalco—you know I wouldn't do a mean thing like that. These nice folks are gonna gimme a part in one of their plays.

QUEENIE. This was just a rehearsal.

ROSIE. You gonna play somebody dead?

QUEENIE. She was Juliet.

ROSIE. Juliet who?

DESMOND. Is it possible you don't know *Romeo and Juliet*?

ROSIE. They live around here?

DESMOND. It's a famous play by Shakespeare.

ROSIE. He live around?

QUEENIE. Do you know, Miss Montefalco—if that's your name— you really ought to go on one of those afternoon T.V. quiz shows. You're just the type they adore. If you can count up to ten—you can win a fortune.

ROSIE. Well—thank you.

DESMOND. We are very interested in Miss Kronkie's future. We think she has an enormous potential.

OPAL. They're gonna make me a actress, Rosie. An' I ain't never forgot how excitin' it is to be standin' up on a stage—even as a tree.

ROSIE. Well, why didn't you explain whin I come in!

OPAL. I couldn't. I wuz dead.

ROSIE. Jes' goes to prove my cards wuz right. The Queen of Hearts *said* you wuz gonna die an' you did. Queens don't lie. You kin trust a queen.

QUEENIE. Thank you.

OPAL. Well, at least I kin stop worryin' now. I'll be alive fer your birthday.

ROSIE. Is that gonna be my present?

OPAL. Better 'n that. You wait fer tomorrer when you're 49.

ROSIE. Forty-eight. I'm backin' up.

QUEENIE. So now you can go home and we'll continue with our rehearsal.

ROSIE. I ain't in no hurry.

DESMOND. But we never allow anyone to see our auditions. Sorry.

ROSIE. An' you kin make enyone a actress—even Opal?

DESMOND. Indubitably.

ROSIE. Well, ef that means yes—could you make a actress of *me*. I always had a secret dream of goin' on the stage myself.

DESMOND. I'll keep you in mind.

ROSIE. (*To Opal.*) I'll bet you never knew I'd been on the stage whin I wuz young, did you Opal?

OPAL. No!

ROSIE. Yes.

OPAL. No!

ROSIE. Yes. I can still hear all them people yellin' an' clappin'!

OPAL. Where?

ROSIE. In a parade. I was on a float.

OPAL. No!

ROSIE. Yes.

OPAL. Here?

ROSIE. No—before my folks had to leave Genoa. I was Miss Northern Italy.

OPAL. What wuz the parade for, dearie? Columbus?

ROSIE. The Mafia.

OPAL. The Mafia!

ROSIE. No one tole us. That's how we came to come to America.

(*To Desmond.*) I still got my costume. I could put it on fer you.

DESMOND. Some other time.

QUEENIE. No, King—that might be a good idea. Let her go home and get her costume. Meanwhile, we'll go on with our rehearsal here.

DESMOND. Yes—of course. Go home and get your costume. Take your time. We'll be busy here.

ROSIE. Oh, Opal—wouldn't it be won'erful if we wuz in a play together—Montefalco and Kronkie.

OPAL. Well, I already got one profession—I don't know if I could handle two.

ROSIE. I wouldn't hesitate one minute to give up my Hot Meatball Stand fer the theater.

QUEENIE. Let's hope we never have to face that.

ROSIE. Well, I'll go git my costume. Oh, ain't this excitin'. (*Starts for door.*) I'll be right back. You wait for me now. (*Goes out.*)

OPAL. Won'erful woman—that Rosie. Real gen-u-wine. Married a no good dwarf. Met him at a carnival. Imagine a husband no higher than yore knee. Do you know he could run between her legs with two inches to spare.

DESMOND. Yes. Yes—but back to *Romeo and Juliet.* (*The door bursts open and Rosie races in.*)

ROSIE. Shall I bring my sword?

QUEENIE. Your *what*?

ROSIE. On the float, I carried a wooden sword.

QUEENIE. What a co-incidence. She had a wooden sword and you played a tree.

ROSIE. I guess I better bring the sword. I'd feel naked without it. (*She dashes out again.*)

DESMOND. Now, where shall we start again?

QUEENIE. Let's skip the long speech and just start where Juliet says, "Romeo—this do I drink to thee." And then drinks the potion. (*Again the door bursts open and Rosie returns.*)

ROSIE. Shall I dress up at home or dress here?

QUEENIE. Why not at home. I'm sure you have a mirror.

ROSIE. That's right. Opal's is cracked.

QUEENIE. Which doesn't surprise me.

DESMOND. Yes—put on your costume at home and take your time.

OPAL. You do that, dearie. You ain't gonna make a good impression unbuttoned.

34

ROSIE. All right. I'll change at home. Take me longer but don't git nervous. I'll be back. (*Dashes out.*)

OPAL. You'd shore make her happy ef you could find a place for her.

QUEENIE. Oh, we'll find a place for her—don't worry. Hopefully—a permanent place.

OPAL. Well, that's real sweet of you. Poor dear's had a hard life, that runt husband of hers—

QUEENIE. Never mind him—let's get back to Juliet. (*Rosie returns again.*)

ROSIE. It's me again.

QUEENIE. Oh, what now!

ROSIE. I fergot to tell you. Whin I wuz on this float—I held a sword up with one han' an' blew a bugle with the other.

DESMOND. Fine! Bring the bugle.

ROSIE. I cain't. I lost it.

QUEENIE. Then just bring the sword. We'll find a use for it.

OPAL. Rosie, yore gettin' all excited an' you'll git the hiccups. Why don't you jes' set down an' be calm an' I'll fine a costume right here fer you.

DESMOND. No—no. I'm sure she'll be more at ease in her original costume.

QUEENIE. We want to see her as the true Miss Northern Italy. Just as she appeared for the Mafia.

ROSIE. Ef you say. (*To Opal.*) I won't run, Opal. Don't you worry about me. I'll skip.

OPAL. Jes' remember, bein' a actress ain't worth a heart attack.

QUEENIE. That's what I keep telling *myself*.

ROSIE. Well, I'm off then. (*At door.*) I'll bring a poem to recite. One of my own. "Genoa, My Genoa." (*She goes out.*)

QUEENIE. Shall we wait or go on or just kneel and pray?

DESMOND. I'll count to ten. Your friend is certainly tenacious.

OPAL. An' she don't give up easy, neither.

DESMOND. Ten. Now—shall we prepare for Juliet's death.

OPAL. Always pays to prepare fer that. We all get to play that scene sooner or later fer real.

DESMOND. Oh, you're so right, Opal. And a rehearsal makes it better.

OPAL. Well, it ain't ever better but at least you don't usually git a second chance, like I'm gittin'.

QUEENIE. Isn't she brilliant, King!

DESMOND. Superb! (*Hands her book.*) Here—start again.

OPAL. Same place?

QUEENIE. Yes. And you did it so beautifully last time.

OPAL. Git set—hold yore hats. (*Reads.*) "Oh— look! Methinks I see my cousin's ghost seekin' out Romeo—who did split—" (*She stops.*)

QUEENIE. What's the matter?

OPAL. Did he really *split* his cousin?

QUEENIE. A figure of speech—not really.

OPAL. I'm glad. Cause if I wuz Juliet, I couldn't love nobody that split a body right in two.

DESMOND. They were more brutal in those days.

QUEENIE. Go on. You have me hypnotized.

OPAL. O.K. (*Reads.*) "—did split his body upon a—" (*To Queenie.*) Now, don't tell me!— "rapier point." (*To Queenie.*) Got it right that time, didn't I?

QUEENIE. Stupendous!

DESMOND. Right out of Actors' Studio.

OPAL. (*Continues.*) "Stay—Tie-balt—stay! Romeo! Come. This do I *drink*. To thee."

DESMOND. Here's your silver chalice. (*Hands her tin cup.*)

QUEENIE. What acting. She'll be a star, Desmond.

OPAL. That reminds me! (*Takes cup.*) Are you a movie fan?

QUEENIE. Isn't every one?

OPAL. Well, I jes' happin' to have the greatest collection of different things that once belonged to famous movie stars anywhere. (*Puts cup down.*) I'll show you. Yore gonna swoon. (*Crosses to get a box.*)

DESMOND. Later, Opal. We mustn't treat a four hundred year old classic lightly. Romeo is waiting for you to die.

OPAL. Well, if he's waited fer four hun'erd years and she ain't dead yit—he kin wait four minutes more.

DESMOND. (*Tries to hand her the tin cup.*) Drink, Opal— drink.

OPAL. In a minute. Nobody should be in a hurry to die. (*Unties box.*) Had a cousin out in Hollywood—Sally Sue Sprinkler— worked as a maid fer lots of movie stars. Never held a job long on account of her stomach.

QUEENIE. You mean she couldn't stomach them? How droll.

DESMOND. Opal—the show must go on. Curtain!

OPAL. No—it wuz *her* stomach—it growled. Dogs barked at her. Her poor stomach grumbled so loud, it made all them movie stars

36

she worked fer, jumpy. So they'd up an' get another maid. But she'd aluz send me these here reminders of all them famous folks that fired her. It got to be a thing with her—collectin' like me.

QUEENIE. Opal—the play's the thing.

DESMOND. Drink, Juliet.

OPAL. Poor Sally Sue Sprinkler—died las' New Year's. Beer truck hit her right on the dot. She wint out as the New Year come in. But I'll look for her in Heaven whin I go.

QUEENIE. Romeo is looking for you here, Juliet.

OPAL. (Lifts up small item.) You know what this here is?

QUEENIE. It looks like a piece of broken bottle.

OPAL. It is. Root beer. But you know what makes it valuable? Robert Redford cut his foot on it.

QUEENIE. Why?

OPAL. My cousin Sally Sue Sprinkler wuz on the beach an' saw him step on it her own se'f. The minute he limped off, she run right down an' grabbed it. (Holds it up.) It's hard to tell now whether that there stain is blood or root beer.

DESMOND. Romeo—come! This do I drink to thee. (Hands her cup.) Here. Drink. Continue.

OPAL. I am. (Holds something up between two fingers.) An' you know what this here is?

QUEENIE. A piece of thread.

DESMOND. And you're breaking the thread of continuity, Opal. Drink.

OPAL. Well, it ain't a thread. It's a hair right off the head of Irene Dunne. You remember her?

QUEENIE. Not her hair.

DESMOND. Drink, Opal, drink.

OPAL. (Holds up small bottle.) An' I'll bet you can't guess what's in this here bottle.

QUEENIE. It looks like rice. What do I win?

OPAL. Well, it ain't rice. It's the original gen-u-ine fingernail clippin's off the very fingers of Greta Garbo her own self. I'll bet there ain't nobody in this whole wide entire world got eny of her clippin's.

QUEENIE. I'd be inclined to agree with you. But shall we get on.

OPAL. I am. (Lifts up a pair of shorts.) You know what these are?

QUEENIE. Men's shorts. At lease I know that.

DESMOND. Bottoms up, Opal.

37

OPAL. Yes, but you don't know who wore 'em.

QUEENIE. Lincoln?

OPAL. Paul Newman.

QUEENIE. The actor!

OPAL. Well, he ain't the Pope.

QUEENIE. Don't tell me *he* had a maid!

DESMOND. Opal—your tea is getting cold.

OPAL. His wife. An' you know what's interestin' about 'em?

QUEENIE. Yes. How your cousin, Miss *Sprinkler*, got them.

OPAL. He got fat. But what makes 'em *really* special is they ain't bin laundered. They're *fresh! Right off Paul Newman's very own hips* hisself!

DESMOND. Miss Kronkie—just think—when you're famous— this *cup* will be a treasure because *you* drank out of it. (*Hands it to her.*) Down the hatch for fame, Opal!

OPAL. (*Takes cup.*) Would you be interested in Rita Moreno's eyelashes? I only got one.

QUEENIE. I am more interested in your Juliet. (*Pats table.*) Your sarcophagus is waiting, Opal.

OPAL. All right, all right. I'll die, sooner or later. Now— (*Picks up book.*) Doan tell me. I remember. At least I think I do.

QUEENIE. (*Points at page.*) There, Opal—there! Electrify us!

OPAL. I got it. Doan worry. Here goes. (*Reads.*) "Romeo— come! This do I *drink* to *thee-ee!*" (*She downs the tea.*) Yore right—it did get cold.

DESMOND. Die, Opal. I mean Juliet.

QUEENIE. Break our hearts, dear. (*Opal staggers around, enjoying her acting again.*) You're headed the wrong way, Opal. Your sarcophagus is stage left, you're stage right.

OPAL. Right! I'm jes givin' it electricity. (*She staggers to table.*)

QUEENIE. That's the right place. Now die, dear.

OPAL. (*Collapses over table.*) I'm a dead duck. (*They quickly lift her feet and cross her hands.*)

QUEENIE. Beautiful—beautiful! I could cry. If she were clasping a Bible, wouldn't she be the perfect Juliet. I couldn't bear it.

OPAL. (*Sits up.*) I got one. (*Gets off table. They try to push her back.*) This here Bible is sumpin' you gotta see. I'll git it. A Chinese Christian give it to me. (*Goes up to cabinet and tosses several items aside in her search.*) Only it ain't in Chinese. It's printed in gen-u-ine American English. But you never seen anything in your whole entire life like this here gen-u-ine Bible, did you? (*She comes back with a tiny book about the size of a gum eraser. She holds it between two fingers.*) Would you believe this is a Bible. Littlest Bible in the whole entire world but it's all in there. You could take this here little Bible into the Supreme Court and swear on it. Makes you believe in fairies, don't it?

QUEENIE. Opal—you're dead!

OPAL. Well, I've risen. That's in the Bible, too.

QUEENIE. We've read it. (*Pushes her down.*)

OPAL. Not in a teensy-weensie Bible like this.

QUEENIE. Well, you're a big talent so *stay dead* and prove it. (*Covers her with the sheet.*)

OPAL. (*Promptly lifts it off.*) This here Chinese feller told me the missionaries in China wuz persecuted ef they wuz caught with a Bible. Had their heads chopped off. So they printed these teeny-weensie Bibles they could swallow—ef they wuz caught and—why am I gittin' sleepy?

QUEENIE. It's your genius beginning to take over.

DESMOND. Sleep, Juliet.

OPAL. Well, I guess a little nap won't hurt me. Good night folks. (*Lies back and pulls sheet up over her.*)

DESMOND. Think "sleep," Opal, while I get in the mood. Sleep! I'll have to meditate a little while myself to feel the true spirit of Romeo in my guts. (*They wait gleefully.*)

QUEENIE. (*After a moment.*) Opal?

DESMOND. (*Whispers.*) Do you think she's asleep?

QUEENIE. Pinch her.

DESMOND. (*Pokes her with a finger.*) No—it's worked. Now, *we've* got to act fast. You go back and look upstairs. I'll search down here. No telling where she put it. (*Queenie starts up the stairs.*) Yell, if you find it.

QUEENIE. I'll try to think like she thinks—if possible.

DESMOND. (*To self.*) Now where in hell is that damned Vander-dam. (*He searches frantically, racing back and forth across stage opening boxes and hurling junk from barrels and cartons. After a moment there is a yell from upstairs.*) Eureka! She's found it! (*Queenie comes racing down still screaming.*) Shut up! I said *yell* —not scream.

QUEENIE. (*Lifts her hand. It is caught in a large rat trap.*) My hand is caught in a rat trap.

DESMOND. Be quiet. Do you want to wake the dead!

QUEENIE. Get it off—get it off!

DESMOND. (*Releases her hand.*) What did you stick your hand in a rat trap for!

QUEENIE. That's a stupid question. Do you think I did it on purpose? (*Hits him over the head with her purse.*) Why should I want a rat—I married one.

DESMOND. You should have known better. Does it hurt?

QUEENIE. No—it feels good. (*Hits him again.*) I do it all the time for kicks.

DESMOND. Well, don't blame me. I didn't set a rat trap for you.

QUEENIE. Oh, yes you did. Only you offered me an acting job instead of a piece of cheese, I should have taken the cheese.

DESMOND. With seventy-five thousand dollars at stake—it's no time for quibble about rats.

QUEENIE. (*Starts back up stairs.*) All right—all right. You better go into your speech in case she starts to wake up. She's got to think you're acting. (*Exits.*)

DESMOND. (*Resumes search while reciting Romeo's speech.*) "Ah, dear Juliet, why art thou so fair? Shall I believe that insubstantial death is amorous and that the lean abhored monster keeps thee here in the dark to be her paramour? (*Throws clothes out of drawers.*) "For fear that I will stay with thee?" (*Crawls around on his hands and knees peering under cabinets and chairs.*) "And never from this palace of dim night depart again? Here will I remain with worms that are thy chambermaid. (*Goes up to alcove.*) "Oh, here I set my everlasting rest and shake the yoke of inauspicious stars from the world-wearied flesh." (*Queenie comes a few feet down the stairs.*)

QUEENIE. King!

DESMOND. Did you find it!

QUEENIE. No. But do you know what she keeps on the third floor.

DESMOND. A retarded relative?

QUEENIE. Chickens.

DESMOND. What!

QUEENIE. She actually keeps chickens on the third floor.

DESMOND. We're looking for a million-dollar duck and *you* find chickens!

QUEENIE. I just thought you'd like to know. (*Goes back up.*)

DESMOND. Thanks but I'm not hungry. (*Starts search again.*) "Eyes, look your last. Arms, take your last embrace. Come bitter conduct—come unsavory guide, thou desperate pilot, now at once

40

run on the dashing rocks thy sea-sick weary bark—" (*He looks behind cabinet and pulls out the tied up roll of wallpaper.*) The painting! The damned Von Van Vonderdam! Hot damn! (*Races to stairs.*) Queenie—Queenie—come here, quick. Descend—descend.

QUEENIE. (*Comes racing down, hair awry.*) What is it? What have you got?

DESMOND. (*Holds up the roll of wallpaper.*) A million dollar duck.

QUEENIE. The Vanderdam?

DESMOND. The original. (*Starts writing a note.*)

QUEENIE. Did you look at it?

DESMOND. There isn't time.

QUEENIE. How do you know it's the painting?

DESMOND. The rope—it's the same rope.

QUEENIE. What are you doing?

DESMOND. Leaving her a note. And ten dollars. We mustn't steal anything. It's wrong.

QUEENIE. You don't think she's dead, do you?

DESMOND. No—just gullible. Now—let's get out of here quick and collect seventy-five thousand dollars. A reward for our true talent. (*He dashes to door and holds it open.*)

QUEENIE. (*As she goes out.*) My King.

DESMOND. My Queen. (*They go out. There is the sound of a car departing. After a few moments, the door is pushed open. Slowly a sword appears. Then the sound of a human voice imitating a bugle is heard.*)

VOICE. Ta-ta-ta-ta-ta-tata-tata. (*Rosie glides in wearing a flowing red robe and a tinsel crown. She stalks D.C. with sword raised.*)

ROSIE. Behold! Miss Northern Italy! (*When there is no reaction, she looks around.*) Where is everybody?

CURTAIN

ACT THREE

PLACE: *The same.*

TIME: *The next day. Friday morning.*

AT RISE: *Opal is kneeling on the floor beside Gran'ma Kronkie's rocking chair.*

She has a brush and can and is apparently painting the seat.

OPAL. This here ole rocker's bin set in so many years it's a wonder the seat ain't wore out. A lot of human seats has wore out an' gone back to their maker but Gran'ma Kronkie's rocker has outlived all them other behinds that's set in it. It shore kin stan' a good coat of shellac. There's a lot of folks I know could stan' a good shellackin, too, but I'll leave that job to the good Lord—he's a better shellacker than me. Gran'ma Kronkie usta jes' love this here chair. I figure we set her down in this here chair over sixty thousand times before she passed on. That wuz twice a day —once to take her to the outhouse. We'd set her out on the porch in the sun an' she'd sing an' rock *all* day long. People say whin folks git ole, they ain't got many pleasures lef'. That ain't so. There's lots of riches they kin still enjoy—like rockin' an' scratchin' —catchin' flies—waitin' fer the postman—watchin' lizards an' sparrow-hawks—settin' on the toilet—takin' a nap. Why, there's hun'erds of excitin' things they kin still do. An' what they can't —they kin at least remember. We hadda turn her around once in awhile to keep moss from growin' on her north side. Poor ole dear died out there in the sun—jes' stopped rockin'. She'd shrunk so much we buried her in her favorite trunk. Won'erful woman— real gen-u-wine. Had eighteen sons—two born in the cornfield. Lost half of 'em in three world wars—four to liquor—two to Spanish flu an' one to the Baptist ministry. Come spring I aluz plant her favorite flower on her grave—sunflowers. Crows come from everywhere. Won'erful woman. Real gen-u-wine. Deaf as a post. People haf' a mile away could hear us yellin' "Good mornin' " to her. (*She gets up and places the rocker R. out of the way. She crosses back up to the alcove to put brush and can away. There is a knock at the door.*) Kick it open—it ain't locked. (*Rosie enters.*)

42

ROSIE. I bet you think I jes' come over fer a birthday present whin as a matter of fac' I thoroughly an' completely an' fully an' absolutely fergot all about it. Could I borrow a cup of sugar?

OPAL. Well, it don't matter, dearie. Yore here. An' I got a cake fer you.

ROSIE. (*Disappointed.*) Jes' a cake?

OPAL. Jes' for starters. Congratulations fer havin' made it safe an' sound to forty-nine again, Rosie dear.

ROSIE. Forty-eight.

OPAL. Well, I don't know enyone has forty-eight candles so I'm jes' using *one*—same as las' year. Same candle.

ROSIE. Well, actually an' matter of fac', it don't really matter. Whin you git to my age you jes' look forward to one year at a time.

OPAL. Now that ain't thinkin optomistic, Rosie. There's no reason you kaint live to be a hun'erd an' fifty. Turtles do.

ROSIE. Well, I ain't exactly lookin' forward to bein' an old turtle. But thanks, enyways.

OPAL. Set down while I fix you some tea an' git yore birthday present. (*Gets two tin cups and makes tea.*)

ROSIE. Whadda you suppose happined to them actors yestidy—disappeared into thin air. I felt like a fool on the highway in a red dress an' carryin' a sword. Three trucks tried to pick me up.

OPAL. I dunno. They lef' a note sayin' thank you an' ten dollars. Wuzn't that nice of 'em. I'm shore they'll be back.

ROSIE. But why do you suppose they hadda leave in sech a hurry?

OPAL. Maybe they couldn't fin' the bathroom. (*Puts cup down.*) Here—drink yer birthday tea. I used a bran' new bag.

ROSIE. I kain't say my birthday is started out good. I got a leak in my roof—a kink in my back an' ants in my sugar.

OPAL. Did you consult yore fortune cards?

ROSIE. First thing—before I even got dressed.

OPAL. Whad' they say?

ROSIE. Go back to bed.

OPAL. What about yore horoscope? Did you read that?

ROSIE. That didn't hep neither. It says today I shouldn't take no ocean voyage, buy a dog—git married or lend money.

OPAL. Well, that wuz jes' tellin' you what *not* to do. Didn't it tell you enything you *should* do?

ROSIE. Yes. Go back to bed.

OPAL. (*Rises.*) Well, you'll feel better when you see what *I* got fer yore birthday. First, yore birthday cake. (*She goes to the alcove and brings back a cake with one used candle. She places it on a high stool beside the table.*) There! All fer you, sweetheart.

ROSIE. Looks like cocoanut.

OPAL. It is. Baked it myse'f las' night.

ROSIE. (*Sadly.*) Oh. Sorry you wint to all that trouble.

OPAL. Don't you like cocoanut?

ROSIE. Gives me gas.

OPAL. Well, honey—it ain't no trouble to scrape it off. I'll save it fer another cake. It ain't wasted.

ROSIE. What kinder cake is underneath?

OPAL. (*Proudly.*) Chocolate layer.

ROSIE. (*Again morosely.*) Oh. I wish you'd tole me.

OPAL. Don't you like chocolate neither?

ROSIE. Oh, yes—I like it all right. It jes' don't like me.

OPAL. Drat! I shoulda ast you. That's the trouble with surprises —you git surprised. (*Rises and crosses to alcove.*) Well, wait'll you see yore *real* present. That'll make up fer the cocoanut. (*Returns with package.*) An' here's yore present. Happy birthday, Rosie dear.

ROSIE. What's in it?

OPAL. Well, you gotta open it an' see.

ROSIE. Pretty paper. You buy it?

OPAL. Shore did. Ain't nothin' too good fer my bes' fren'.

ROSIE. (*Starts unwrapping present.*) It's kinda long. Hope it ain't sumpin' I hafta plant.

OPAL. It ain't.

ROSIE. Or put together myself.

OPAL. It's sumpin' to remind you of them happy days when you lived on yore farm.

ROSIE. I hope you don't mean a calendar. Four months is already gone by.

OPAL. I'll give you a hint. Quack-quack. What does that remind you of?

ROSIE. A couple of doctors.

OPAL. Think of a kinda beak with yeller eyes close together.

ROSIE. My cousin Louisa Gucci?

OPAL. With feathers.

ROSIE. That could still be Louisa.

OPAL. (*Beams.*) I guess you'll jes' hafta unroll it an' see. (*Rosie unrolls the canvas. She stares at it. She hurls it back on the table and bursts into tears.*)

ROSIE. Oh, no—no! Not on my birthday!

OPAL. Rosie—what in thunder is the matter?

ROSIE. That "pitchure"! As if things ain't bad enough. (*Puts her head down and sobs.*)

OPAL. Rosie—what's wrong with the "pitchure"? Don't you like it?

ROSIE. Like it! I hate it. How could you do this to me? You—my fren'—givin' me a pitchure to remind me of my poor little pet duck Donald that got squashed by a truck. An' hangin' upside down, too.

OPAL. Oh, Rosie, honey, I never thought of it that way. Oh, ain't I a fool. (*Picks up broom.*) Here—hit me with somethin'!

ROSIE. No—I know you never meant to break my heart—not on my birthday. But that's what you done.

OPAL. I wish I wuz dead.

ROSIE. No—Donald bein' dead is bad enough. Do you think I could look at that awful "pitchure" every day an' not be reminded of Donald? I'd cry every time rememberin' how I usta put a grain of corn between my teeth and he'd take it out—gentle—jes' like he wuz kissin' me. (*She sobs violently.*)

OPAL. (*Pats her.*) Rosie, sweetheart—lemme give you sumpin' else. Enything! (*Reaches into barrel.*) Here. How about a beaded purse.

ROSIE. What do I need with a purse on what I make.

OPAL. Well—here. (*Finds a substitute.*) How about a fly swatter. That's somethin' enybody kin use.

ROSIE. You think that's very nice—hintin' that I got flies? On my birthday? Ants is bad enough.

OPAL. I'm tryin', honey—I'm tryin'. (*Lifts mug.*) Here's a nice beer mug.

ROSIE. (*Rises and starts for door.*) I don't drink my milk in no beer mug.

OPAL. (*Pursues her.*) How about this here shawl—it's very Italian.

ROSIE. (*At door.*) Never mind. I'll jes' go home an' spen' my birthday takin' ants outta my sugar. (*She goes out. Opal hurls the shawl back into a barrel and comes Down to face audience.*)

OPAL. Now ain't that the limit. Someone tole me a story once a long time ago that I ain't never fergot. Some of you may know it but good advice is alwuz worth repeatin'. Seems like there wuz someone visitin' one of them insane asylums an' they come to a cell

45

where a man had his hat on sideways an' his han' in his vest an' the visitor asts "what's wrong with him?" An' the warden, he sez— "He thinks he's Napoleon." So they come to the next cell where a man with glasses on is runnin' up an' down yellin' "Charge! Remember the *Maine*" and the warden explains "Now this man thinks he's Teddy Roosevelt." But the next cell they come to had padded walls an' a poor feller in a strait-jacket wuz chained to the wall. An' the visitor asts "What's wrong with that poor man?" An' the warden says "Oh, that's a man who tried to please everybody." I hope you git the point. (*She picks up the canvas and looks at it.*) This dern "pitchure's" caused me so much trouble I think I'll jes' put it in my trash and burn it. (*She sticks it into a barrel. She then crosses to the door and starts putting on her various overcoats.*) I'll try an' fine sumpin' fer Rosie in town today while I'm makin' my rounds. But what kin you give a woman who don't use makeup—lipstick—makes her own soap an' uses vanilla fer perfume. (*She takes her little wagon and goes out. After a moment, Desmond and Queenie tiptoe in from the kitchen. Desmond crosses to the door and peeps out.*)

DESMOND. She's gone. Didn't even look back.

QUEENIE. Some crook you are—stealing a roll of wallpaper instead of that Dutch masterpiece. (*She throws the roll against the wall.*)

DESMOND. All right—so it wasn't the missing "Mallard and Apple." Everybody makes mistakes. Even Adam and Eve.

QUEENIE. At least they knew an apple when they saw it.

DESMOND. And who was it stuck her hand in a rat trap?

QUEENIE. Look—let's not stop to bicker here—we can do that at home. We want to find that damned Vanderdam.

DESMOND. Then you start upstairs—room by room—and I'll start in the basement.

QUEENIE. (*Starts up the stairs.*) If you find it—don't you dare go off and leave me holding the sack.

DESMOND. Do you think I'd do that to you?

QUEENIE. For seventy-five thousand dollars, you'd do it to your grandmother. (*She goes Up out of sight.*)

DESMOND. Lizzie Borden rides again. (*He goes to basement door in the alcove under the stairs and disappears. After a moment, the front door opens and Opal returns.*)

OPAL. It's a cryin' shame science ain't come up with a brain transplant, I could shore use one. Now, how come I didn't think to take my cake with me. (*She stops beside it on the stool.*) I'll jes' cut it inta slices an' give a piece to all my fren's I pass on the highway goin' into town. Think I'll jes' leave the candle on fer dressin'. (*Looks around.*) Now where'd I put that knife I wuz goin' to cut it up with? Musta left it in the kitchen. What a brain! (*She goes into the kitchen. Desmond comes up from the basement.*) DESMOND. She *must* have a flashlight or a candle around some place. (*He searches the alcove and finds matches. He sees the cake.*) Ah—a candle. (*He takes the candle and goes back into the basement. Opal returns with a knife. She crosses to the cake.*) OPAL. Well, I coulda swore I had a candle in that cake. I musta took it in the kitchen. (*She puts the knife down and returns to the kitchen. Desmond comes up from the basement.*) DESMOND. All those damn boxes tied with rope. (*Sees knife.*) Ah—just what I need. (*He disappears into the basement with the knife. Opal returns. She stares down at the cake.*) OPAL. Now, where'd I put that knife? (*Shakes her head resignedly and starts back for kitchen.*) Ef I ain't careful, I'm gonna git run over. (*Goes into kitchen. Desmond comes up from the basement.*) DESMOND. A ladder—my kingdom for a ladder. (*Sees stool.*) Ah—this will do just as well. (*He transfers the cake to a sideboard and takes the stool down to the basement. Opal returns with another knife. She stares down where the stool had been. She sees the cake on the sideboard. She sits down.*) OPAL. Well, I guess it's happened at last. You git older before you know it an' git what them doctors call see-*nile*-ity. You start forgettin' things—then places—then people. I seen it happen to Gran'ma Kronkie—couldn't remember where she lef her glasses. Next she started forgittin' people—didn't know who nobody wuz. I kin remember like it wuz yestidy that mornin' I took her breakfast in an' she thought I wuz a turkey. Broke my heart. An' now it's started happenin' to me. They say a dog's memory is about as long as whatever you hit him with. Well, mine ain't even that long. Guess what I need is a good dog. (*Rises.*) Well, I'll give it one more try. I'll put this here knife back an' see ef I kin remember it's in the kitchen. (*She goes into kitchen. Desmond comes up from the basement with the stool. He replaces it where it was and returns the cake and also replaces the candle. He puts the knife beside the cake and goes back down into basement. Opal returns from the kitchen and halts in front of the cake.*) Now, I know I'm

47

losin' my mine. Or maybe there ain't nothing there at all an' I jes' imagine I see a cake there. At least it ain't a turkey. (*She sticks her finger into the cake and tastes her finger.*) Chocolate. It's mine all right. Could be sweeter. Well, I know what's wrong with me now. It's that banana ice cream I et on top of sauerkraut. All I need is a couple of aspirin. (*Starts for stairs.*) How many times have I got to remin' myself that the bes' person to make a fool of you, is yoreself. (*Halfway up the stairs she turns, in her customary manner, to back up the remaining steps. Above her, Queenie has started down, sees Opal and flees back up the stairs. When both have disappeared, Desmond comes back up from the basement, dusting his hands.*)

DESMOND. That's not a basement. It's the Smithsonian Museum —with dust. (*He stops beside the cake and looks down at it.*) Why not? I can use the energy. (*He picks up the knife and cuts himself a small piece. He gulps it and is licking his fingers as Queenie tiptoes in from the kitchen behind him. She taps him on the shoulder, sending him leaping into the air.*) Don't do that! I've got a weak bladder.

QUEENIE. She's here!

DESMOND. Who's here!

QUEENIE. Opal. She came back.

DESMOND. Where is she?

QUEENIE. Upstairs. I saw her just in time and came down the back stairs.

DESMOND. Did she see you?

QUEENIE. Not unless she's got eyes in the back of her head—which I doubt.

DESMOND. What'll we do?

QUEENIE. Hit her over the head with something.

DESMOND. What! A teabag?

QUEENIE. (*Looks frantically around.*) She must have an old tire iron or tennis racket. (*Points to alcove.*) Look! Isn't that a baseball bat?

DESMOND. I don't know. I never played. (*They dash up to the alcove and take a bat out of an umbrella stand.*)

QUEENIE. It's a bat.

DESMOND. And she's a bat. They belong together.

QUEENIE. Can you do it?

DESMOND. For seventy-five thousand dollars I'd play ball with the devil.

QUEENIE. We'll hide here and when she passes, crack down.

DESMOND. I wish I'd played ball when I was a kid. I wouldn't be so nervous.

QUEENIE. Were you too poor?

DESMOND. No. I was a sissy.

QUEENIE. You can't miss. Her head is bigger than a baseball— and twice as dense.

DESMOND. Shh! I think she's comin' down. (*They hide out of sight on the alcove platform. Opal comes down the stairs.*)

OPAL. Lucky thing I remembered where I put them aspirin. Bes' way to keep asperin fresh is put 'em in a match-box and seal 'em in a pickle jar. Las' forever. *As she crosses to cake.*) Shore glad it wuz my stomach an' not my brain. (*She looks down and sees a slice of cake missing.*) Mice. Can't turn yore back enymore in here. (*Desmond and Queenie step down behind Opal. He raises the bat. Before he can bring it down, Opal turns and crosses to door. Desmond and Queenie follow behind her—bat raised. When she stops beside the door, they get up on the first step and raise the bat to hit her. She bends over however to pick up a cardboard carton. Desmond hides the bat behind him.*) This here oughta hold the cake. (*She returns to the stool, leaving them stranded on the step. They look at each other helplessly. Opal turns and sees them. They grin sheepishly.*) Well, look who's here. Fer heaven's sake, I never heard you come in. I mus' be gittin' deaf too. Come in— come in. Glad to see you folks. I wuz wonderin' whin you'd come back.

QUEENIE. (*Regains her wits first.*) Oh, we—we were out this way and thought we'd drop in.

OPAL. Well, you almos' missed me. I wuz Jes' goin' out agin.

DESMOND. We wanted to explain yesterday. Queenie became suddenly ill and we couldn't wake you—you were such a convincing Juliet.

QUEENIE. Such reality! Such truth!

OPAL. Well, it wuz mighty kind of you to leave that note an' the ten bucks. Set down an' have a piece of cake.

QUEENIE. Well, we only have a few minutes. Did you say you were just going out?

OPAL. Well, not now I got guests. I'll wait till you folks havta go first.

QUEENIE. Oh, don't let us detain you.

OPAL. You won't. An' I'm shore glad you come back because I

found somethin' I wanna give you as a present, you bin so nice to me. (*Gets large box and takes it to table. Desmond and Queenie cross to stand behind her.*)

DESMOND. How very kind of you. It hits me—here. (*Hits his heart.*)

QUENNIE. What is it? (*Opal takes a smaller box out of the big box. Desmond raises the bat. Before he can strike, Opal puts the first box on the floor.*)

OPAL. It's somepin' you ain't never seen before an' even whin you see it you ain't gonna believe it. (*She takes a third box out of the second box. And again Desmond raises his bat only to be foiled as she bends to put second box on the floor.*)

QUEENIE. This delay is killing me. (*Opal takes a progressively smaller box out of the third box.*)

OPAL. I wanna surprise you.

DESMOND. You're succeeding.

OPAL. Havin' it in lots of boxes builds up suspense, don't it?

DESMOND. True—true. You hit it on the head. (*He raises the bat. Opal stoops to put the third empty box down.*)

OPAL. I hope this ain't holdin' you folks up.

QUEENIE. Oh, not at all. We intend to stay with you. (*Opal takes a fifth small box out of the last one.*)

OPAL. It'll be worth it at the end.

DESMOND. We're counting on that. (*He raises the bat. Again Opal bends to place boxes on floor into each other.*)

QUEENIE. Oh, don't tell me there's a box in that box.

DESMOND. We've already gone past our curtain.

OPAL. Well, this is it. Here you are! (*She takes a pin cushion out of the last box.*)

QUEENIE. A pin cushion?

OPAL. But lookie there. This one's got a pin in it. One pin.

QUEENIE. We've been held up by a pin.

OPAL. Oh, but you never seen a pin like this. You know what's writ on the head of this pin? The Lord's Prayer. (*As Desmond raises his bat, Opal moves away.*) But you gotta have a magnifying glass to read it. (*Returns with magnifying glass.*)

QUEENIE. How can anyone write the Lord's Prayer on the head of a pin!

OPAL. An angel, I guess. Look—now ain't that won'erful. Here— put yore head next to mine. (*With their heads together, Opal starts reading.*)

"Our Father which art in heaven,
Hallowed be thy name."
(*Desmond raises bat.*)
"Thy kingdom come, thy will be done—
On earth as it is in heaven."
It's all there.
(*Continues reading. Desmond cannot bring himself to strike, and lowers bat.*)
"Lead us not into temptation but deliver us from evil,
For thine is the kingdom an' the power an' the glory. Amen."
(*Turns to Queenie.*) Ain't that won'erful? An' yore sech won'erful folks yoreselves, I want you to have it as a present. (*Puts it in Queenie's hands.*) Lemme git you some string to tie the boxes. (*She goes into kitchen.*)
QUEENIE. (*Angrily.*) Why didn't you hit her!
DESMOND. While she's saying the Lord's Prayer? God would strike me dead.
QUEENIE. Well, if He doesn't—*J* will.
DESMOND. I may be an actor but I've got some scruples.
QUEENIE. When we get that seventy-five thousand is plenty of time for scruples.
DESMOND. Stop getting nervous—you're making me nervous.
QUEENIE. Give me the bat—I'll do it. (*Opal comes back to see them struggling over the bat.*)
OPAL. Oh, I see you foun' that famous bat. Belonged to Joe DiMaggio. You heard of him?
QUEENIE. Yes. He knew how to hit.
OPAL. (*To Desmond.*) You play baseball?
QUEENIE. He just took it up.
OPAL. Well, in that case, I'll make you a present of the bat, too. You kin practice.
QUEENIE. He needs it.
DESMOND. Too bad we can't have what we really want—that painting.
OPAL. You mean that dead duck?
QUEENIE. Yes—"Mallard and Apple."
OPAL. Well, you know—it's a funny thing about that "pitchure." I wuz savin' it fer my fren's birthday but she bust right into tears. Reminded her of a pet duck she once had. You'd a thought I done it on purpose to make her unhappy. Almos' threw it back in my face.

QUEENIE. You mean—it's available?
DESMOND. You still have it!
OPAL. Shore. It's right here. (*Takes it out of barrel.*) She didn't want no part of it.
DESMOND. I'll give you seven hundred dollars for it right now.
OPAL. No. I've made up my mine. I ain't gonna let nobody have it fer no seven hun'erd.
DESMOND. Eight hundred.
OPAL. No. Because it ain't worth that. An' I ain't about to cheat nobody.
DESMOND. All right—five hundred.
OPAL. No. It's too much. An' ef there's one thing I got—it's scruples.
DESMOND. Four hundred.
OPAL. No—I ain't gonna let nobody make no crook outta me.
QUEENIE. Three hundred.
OPAL. Why I'd feel like a thief.
DESMOND. Two hundred.
OPAL. The good Lord would strike me dead.
QUEENIE. One hundred.
OPAL. I got my pride an' it ain't fer sale for a hun'erd.
DESMOND. Seventy-five dollars.
QUEENIE. Fifty.
DESMOND. Twenty-five and that's our lowest bid.
QUEENIE. (*Kicks him.*) Fifteen.
OPAL. (*Hesitates.*) You folks don't un'erstan'. Whin yore young you got a lot of differint passions pullin' you this way an' that. But as a body gits older an' more sensible, all them passions ain't as strong—*except one*—greed. Well, since I never had it whin I was young—it's a little late fer me to start supportin' a new vice at my age.
QUEENIE. But you don't understand either. We want to make you *happy*.
OPAL. Well, in that case—I ain't got no choice but to let you have it fer fifteen, though it ain't worth two.
QUEENIE. You will!
OPAL. I give you my word, didn't I? An' I never take a word of mine back unless it's a swear word. (*Hands her the canvas.*)
QUEENIE. Desmond—give her the fifteen—quick. (*Starts across room hugging the painting.*) We got it! We got it! It's ours!
OPAL. I hope you folks realize you're gittin' the most expensive duck you'll ever buy.

52

QUEENIE. Oh, we do . . . we do.

DESMOND. Let's see . . . I have a ten and . . . do you mind five ones?

OPAL. Don't know enyone who does. I hope this ain't gonna run you short. Ten would do.

DESMOND. You said fifteen and that's the deal. I am not one to haggle. *He counts the money ceremoneously.*) Ten . . . and one . . . two . . . three . . . four . . five. And here's an extra quarter to show my goodwill.

OPAL. Why, that shows in yore face, Mister. . . both of you. But I'll take the quarter enyhow fer luck.

QUEENIE. I want you to know, you've made us very happy Thespians, Opal.

OPAL. That's what life is all about, ain't it honey. (*Takes money.*) Thank you kindly . . . an' God forgive me fer robbin' you.

DESMOND. You will be in our thoughts, Opal, whenever we see a duck. Or roast one.

OPAL. Jes' so you don't never have to eat crow.

QUEENIE. Au revoir. That's French for "goodbye."

DESMOND. Auf wiedersehen. That's German for "farewell."

OPAL. Oddgay essblay ouyay. That's pig-latin fer "God bless you." Take care en' have a good day . . . en' that's plain English. (*They go out. Opal turns to the audience.*) Ain't makin folks happy about the mos' rewardin' thing a body kin do? Excep' maybe bakin' a good cake. An' ain't it reassurin' to know the world is jes' full of good folks you kin trust? Why, I'll bet enyone a dime ef you wuz to take all yore money en' give it to ten people to invest fer you, not one single solitary one of 'em would cheat you. (*Lets this sink in.*) Unless they wuz rich. (*Rosie enters.*)

ROSIE. Opal, them acter fren's of yourn' jes' now like to have run over me.

OPAL. Maybe they wuz lookin' at their mallard an' it was up to you to duck. (*Laughs uproariously at her pun.*)

ROSIE. You mean to say you sole 'em that pitchure?

OPAL. Paid me a fortune fer it.

ROSIE. You seen today's paper?

OPAL. Now. Rosie, you know I never read no paper until it's too late to do enything about it.

ROSIE. Well, that may be jes' what you've did. How much did you git fer it?'

OPAL. Fifteen smackers plus two bits.

ROSIE. You sole it fer fifteen bucks and twenty-five cents!

OPAL. That's right. Why?

ROSIE. Do you know how much that there dead duck is worth?

OPAL. About two bucks.

ROSIE. Listen to this here. (*Reads.*) "The Missing Million Dollar Masterpiece 'Mallard and Apple' which was thought to be lost was discovered last night in the museum vault to the great relief of the insurance company which had offered a seventy-five thousand dollar reward for its recovery. It was revealed also that a worthless copy had been made by a museum artist who was requested to discard it, which was done." (*Rosie looks up.*) That's the one you found, Opal. An' fifteen dollars! Opal, you cheated a couple of innocent actors outta their hard-earned money actin'. You ortta be ashamed.

OPAL. Oh, I feel jes' terrible. I robbed 'em, didn't I?

ROSIE. Well, it's bin a terrible day—an' my birthday, too. I ain't surprised. (*Starts for door.*)

OPAL. Rosie—wait. Lemme give you sumpin'. Here—you take this money they give me as a birthday present.

ROSIE. No—I don't want no tainted money—not on my birthday.

OPAL. (*Picks up vase.*) How about a nice glass vase to put yore paper flowers in? Look nice on yore hot meat ball counter.

ROSIE. No. I use a ketsup bottle.

OPAL. It's real crystal.

ROSIE. (*Opens door.*) Never mind. I'll— (*Stops.*) What'd you say?

OPAL. I said it wuz real crystal.

ROSIE. (*Brightens and shut door.*) Crystal! That wuz my *mother's* name.

OPAL. Yore mother's name wuz Crystal? Why Rosie Montefalco —what a co-in-*side*-ence. Crystal!

ROSIE. (*Returns.*) Yes. My mother's name wuz—(*She fondles vase.*) Crystal da Vinci Leonardo Magnani Baptisti Cellini Mercutio Puccini Montefalco Smith.

OPAL. Smith!

ROSIE. She married agin whin my father got killed in a Peace Rally.

OPAL. Then take that vase, Rosie. Only it's called "vahz." Over five bucks, it's a vahz. An' take the flowers, too. You like tulips, don't you?

ROSIE. No. I had tulips at my weddin'. I wilted before they did. (*She goes out.*)

OPAL. (*Calls after her.*) Well, have a happy birthday, dearie.

An' remember your horror-scope—don't take no ocean voyage or buy a dog. (*She closes the door and turns to the audience with a happy smile.*) Well, folks, it jes' goes to prove everything turns out fer the best ef you jes' *wait* long enough. Take my grandma Kronkie—she loved her ole rockin' chair. An' she died there—settin' up—got her wish—didn't hafter take off her clothes to die. An' we didn't hafter put 'em on to bury her. Things alluz work out—even ef it does take a hunerd an' five years, six months, three days an' twenty minutes. So now I'll leave you on that encouragin' thought. Odgay essblay ouyay—an' that's pig latin for "God Bless You."

CURTAIN

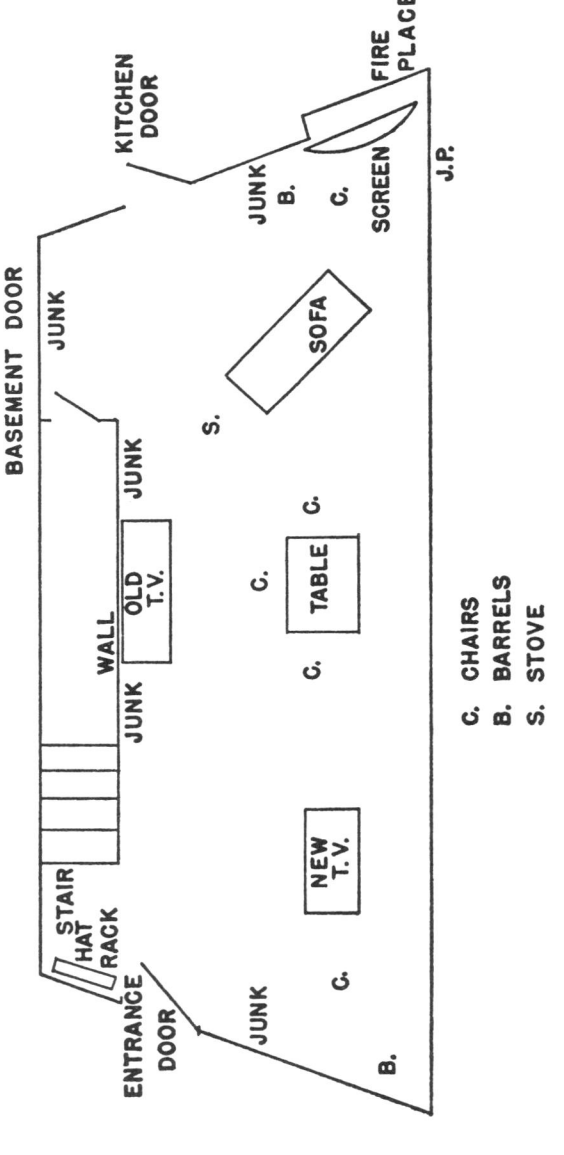

SCENE DESIGN

"OPAL'S MILLION DOLLAR DUCK"

C. CHAIRS
B. BARRELS
S. STOVE

PROPERTY LIST

ACT ONE

Painting of "Mallard and Apple"
Small wagon
Rope and pulley
Various "junk" articles
Playing cards
String of tea bags
Kettle and tin cups
Medicine bottle
Rocking chair
Barrels
Cane
Cigarettes and matches
Teddy bear
Theatre ticket
Necklace
Cape (Dracula)
Sequined gown
Spanish comb
Bed sheets
Feather boa
Muff
Newspaper
Small trunk of paper money
Floppy hat with ribbons
Ear muffs

ACT TWO

Roll of wallpaper
Tulips
Copy of "Romeo and Juliet"
Bed sheet, in tin box
Crystal vase
Wrapping paper
Small bottle and eye dropper
Several eye glasses
Broken piece of glass
Thread of hair

Men's shorts
Small bottle of "nail clippings"
Miniature Bible
Large rat trap
Red costume, tinsel crown & wooden sword

ACT THREE

Stool
Cake and candle
Paint can and brush
Wrapping paper and cord
Beaded purse
Fly swatter
Beer mug
Spanish shawl
Baseball bat
Kitchen knives
Various incongruous articles
    in barrels for Desmond's search
Various incongruous articles in barrels for Desmond's search
Broom
Matches
Nest of five boxes, with pin cushion in last box
Pin, in pin cushion
Magnifying glass
Money (bills and coins)

NEW
PLAYS

THE GRAPES OF WRATH
AUGUST SNOW
NIGHT DANCE
BETTER DAYS
THE WIDOW'S BLIND DATE
SOUTHERN CROSS
THREE POETS
MOUNTAIN LANGUAGE
ELLIOT LOVES
COBB
TO FORGIVE, DIVINE
THE POPE'S NOSE
OPERA COMIQUE
TREASURE ISLAND

Write for information as to
availability
DRAMATISTS PLAY SERVICE, Inc.
440 Park Avenue South   **New York, N.Y. 10016**

NEW
PLAYS

SIX DEGREES OF SEPARATION
SPUNK
TWO ROOMS
ANTHONY ROSE
ABUNDANCE
MOUNTAIN
¿DE DONDE?
INCOMMUNICADO
YANKEE DAWG YOU DIE
ABOUT TIME
THE DEAL
IMAGINING BRAD
MURDER IN GREEN MEADOWS
CAHOOTS

Write for information as to
availability
DRAMATISTS PLAY SERVICE, Inc.
440 Park Avenue South   New York, N.Y. 10016

NEW
PLAYS

BREAKING LEGS

STATES OF SHOCK

THE LITTLE TOMMY PARKER CELEBRATED
COLORED MINSTREL SHOW

VEINS AND THUMBTACKS

FRIDAYS

STAY CARL STAY

BEST HALF-FOOT FORWARD

PILLOW TALK

THAT SERIOUS HE-MAN BALL

A CHRISTMAS CAROL

FOREPLAY: OR THE ART OF THE FUGUE

*Write for information as to
availability*
DRAMATISTS PLAY SERVICE, Inc.
440 Park Avenue South   New York, N.Y. 10016